Rescued!

Tales of California Canine Rescue

Stories of compassion, courage, renewed health, and happiness for rescued canines

By Julie Anne Schubert

http://www.doersofgood.com

iUniverse, Inc.
New York, New York
Bloomington, Indiana

Rescued!
Tales of California Canine Rescue

The views expressed in this work are solely those of the author and do not necessarily reflect the views of the publisher, and the publisher hereby disclaims any responsibility for them.

iUniverse books may be ordered through booksellers or by contacting:

iUniverse
1663 Liberty Drive
Bloomington, IN 47403
www.iuniverse.com
1-800-Authors (1-800-288-4677)

Because of the dynamic nature of the Internet, any Web addresses or links contained in this book may have changed since publication and may no longer be valid.

ISBN: 978-1-4502-6121-0 (sc)
ISBN: 978-1-4502-6123-4 (dj)
ISBN: 978-1-4502-6122-7 (ebk)

Printed in the United States of America

iUniverse rev. date: 10/19/2010

This book is dedicated to the untold number of unpaid and overworked volunteers, Doers of Good, who rescue and rehabilitate lost, injured, and homeless dogs, and to all dogs in shelters still waiting to be rescued.

A very special thanks to my loving family, who understood the importance of this project and supported it every step of the way.

Acknowledgments

Our cover is that of gentile Minoo, the 500th dog saved by Muttville's Senior Dog Rescue from East Los Angeles, where she was used for many years as a breeder for a puppy mill. She was covered in ticks and didn't know how to lie in a dog bed. In two days she blossomed into a curious, playful, tail-wagging sweetheart!

We want to thank professional photographer Mark Rogers in San Francisco for providing us with a wonderful cover, and for his amazing work with canine rescue organizations and shelters in the San Francisco Bay Area. His Web site is http://www.markrogersphotography.com.

Also, thanks to all of the current owners and rescue organizations for the photographs accompanying the stories; and in particular Jeff Pokonsky for the picture of Jake, Chris Perondi for the picture of Action Jackson, and Phil Slattery for the picture of Marbo.

Table of Contents

Introduction

Unless someone like you cares a whole awful lot, nothing is going to get better. It's not. —Dr. Seuss

Every second of every minute of every day, a helpless animal is put to death, just because no one was there to take them home. —Unknown

Welcome to the world of canine rescue! Did you know that on any given day in the state of California there are tens of thousands of unpaid and overworked volunteers—doers of good—who rescue and rehabilitate unfortunate dogs trapped in county shelters, lost on the streets, or those given up? As organized rescue organizations, the doers seek to minimize the suffering that occurs from abandonment, abuse, violence, isolation, hunger, despair, fear, injury, and infection, and heal by unconditional love, compassion, kindness, food, shelter, medical care, and physical and emotional rehabilitation.

Since the 1980s there has been an explosion of volunteer rescue organizations for most breeds in *all* major cities in the United States. Why? Staggering numbers of adoptable pets are euthanized in shelters due to overpopulation. National figures now show that approximately four million pets die in shelters every year! Here in California, there's recently been an increase of 30–40 percent of pets turned into shelters; and not surprising, 30–40 percent are put down. Twenty-five percent of them are purebred. There is simply no room and no funding to build bigger shelters.

Despite this massive overpopulation problem and spay/neuter programs, breeders continue to breed. Owners fail to spay and neuter. People seeking dogs continue to buy puppies from pet shops and private breeders, instead of opting for mature dogs available in shelters or rescue organizations. And now, coupled with today's economic woes of bank foreclosures and new financial stress for dog owners, the number of pets turned into California county shelters has taken another turn for the worse. Owners are reportedly abandoning their dogs in back yards, and abused and neglected animals continue to suffer at the hands of clueless, irrational owners.

A local nonkill shelter in Southern California reported in January of 2009 that its number of surrendered cats and dogs during a recent three-month period tripled from that of a year ago. But there is another solution to surrendering animals to county shelters—there are kind-hearted and determined volunteers out there finding their pets new homes through animal rescue organizations.

The purpose of this book is to educate people seeking a dog about the "option for adoption"—a compassionate alternative to buying from breeders—and to stress the importance of owners turning in their dogs to local dog rescue organizations instead of local shelters. Also, we must celebrate the fact that dogs pulled from the shelters by canine rescue groups go on to lead happy, productive, and sometimes amazing lives as best buddies, in-home companions, assisted living dogs, guide dogs for the blind, therapy dogs in hospitals, land/water search and rescue dogs, DEA drug sniffing dogs, law enforcement dogs, agility athletes, media stars of stage and screen, and other exceptional careers. They truly are blessings in our lives.

This book also wants to acknowledge and thank the dedicated and determined rescue volunteers, who put forth their best efforts twenty-four/seven. These very special people are like you and me with very busy lives and full-time jobs. Homemakers, mothers, grandmothers, wives, husbands, students, and retired executives focus on the work needed and donate their spare time on weekdays, nights, and weekends to the cause.

Founded by single, compassionate dog owners and professional canine clubs, canine rescue organizations and sanctuaries have now become lean, mean, marketing- and promotion-savvy, 501(c) (3) tax-exempt nonprofits—from a home office, apartment, or extended garage to a sizeable ranch. Some of the larger agencies are sometimes an extension of a specific dog breed's national organization and are run by boards of directors with designated volunteers in every state of the United States. Creative fundraising and promotion dominate their agendas, and networking opportunities are used like never before with Facebook, Twitter, LinkedIn, and YouTube. Thankfully the Internet has made it possible for an easier facilitation of the rescue process by part-time volunteers. Now virtually all of the organizations have creative and sophisticated Web sites, some with streaming video, that inform and direct people seeking or giving up dogs. They will be led to an application process, the owner turn-in information, and an appropriate volunteer.

In the larger organizations where large metropolitan areas or regions of a state are covered, the rescuers themselves are linked together with e-mail chat rooms. Here they share every day's events and laugh, cry, console, and support each other through rescue after rescue, adoption after adoption, problem after problem, death after death, and miracle after miracle.

Canine rescue is a well-oiled machine with many moving parts. All of these moving parts—from the head of the organization to the driver who transports animals to other parts of the state— have to work together to be effective. It's all about focus and dedication, long hours and late hours, few to no free weekends or holidays. It's about checkbooks, cell phones, cameras, spare collars, spare leashes, blankets, towels, baby wipes, soothing music CDs, roomy backseats, available passenger seats, air-conditioning or heat, water bottles, plastic dishes, dog biscuits, turkey dogs from

Wienerschnitzel, or burgers from McDonald's (hold the bun, cheese, onions, pickles, sauce, lettuce, and tomato). There are many ways to volunteer your time with your favorite organization. Here are some of the many jobs or moving parts in canine rescue:

Shelter photographer/Internet posters are the most critical in terms of showing and posting information on the Internet. They show which animals have arrived at the shelter and the window of time that they are available for adoption. Many canine girls and boys are pulled out and saved on the last day, near the last hour. The volunteer has to endure the sadness and angst of all of the animals in the shelter on a day-to-day basis and photographs/notates all dogs. Despite her/his efforts, many will not make it out.

Rescue agents have a hands-on job requiring ongoing and careful evaluation of dogs needed to be pulled from the shelter from the Internet postings or shelter visits, and the careful planning of when, where, and how. (Sometimes a shelter employee will call at odd hours to tip off the volunteer that a dog is particularly traumatized or in bad physical shape, or kindly suggests the immediate evacuation for the dog's sake.) Using the power of a checkbook, the rescue agent will pay the shelter fees, scoop up the traumatized dog, and drive it to an approved veterinarian's office for an examination and evaluation of injuries, infections/infestations, and given needed vaccinations. There the dog will stay until it can be picked up and placed into the rescue's foster home.

This is an important beginning of the healing process, with kind words and whispers, hugs, water, air-conditioning or heat, and soothing music. More often than not, the canine girl or boy will insist on sitting as close to the rescuer as possible during the drive, and for the bigger dogs sitting in the back seat, a paw might be placed on their healer's shoulder. The dogs are keenly aware that they've been spared and anxiously await their unknown destination.

Kennel-visiting volunteers continue the healing process at the veterinarians' offices by providing needed TLC: walks, potty breaks, gentle touches, hugs, and kind words. Many of the dogs require medical attention, surgeries, and recuperation time, and this may be the beginning of the revival of a dog's spirit.

Foster-care moms and dads open their homes and hearts to the healthy, good-to-go dogs that need forever homes, and for the recuperation or rehabilitation of the ones with physical or emotional problems. Here they get the critical, unconditional love and care that they need to overcome and thrive. Fosters have canine skill sets that involve the teaching of house-training, obedience, manners, and nonaggressive behavior, as well as delivering and caring for puppies. Foster families usually provide dog food and equipment, but the rescue organization reimburses for basic veterinary care.

Family representatives act as liaisons between the available dogs and prospective adoptive homes. Applications, home checks, telephone interviews, and home visits may be facilitated. Family reps decide what sort of home a family would make for a dog, and what type of dog would best fit. They may help the family search for a good match, forwarding information about suitable and available dogs.

Transportation agents help with local transportation, such as driving from the foster home to the vet or the foster home to a "dog showing" at PETCO or PetSmart. They may also work with others as a driving team to send a dog from So Cal to Nor Cal, or vice versa, for placement with another organization.

Babysitters/home issues/obedience training volunteers help with taking a foster dog for a weekend when the foster family is out of town. Sometimes new owners need a little bit of help with getting a dog settled or retrained concerning house-training, barking, digging, or general obedience.

Outreach and public relations representatives continue to let people know that the rescue organizations are here to help, and that they need the public's financial support. Some duties include writing thank-you notes to donors; writing articles and providing artwork for newsletters; writing and designing brochures; writing news releases; and manning adoption booths at fairs and dog shows.

Fundraising volunteers are absolutely crucial, and seek to keep pace with need. Rescues depend on funding for medical expenses that include surgeries, medications, vaccinations, veterinarians' fees, boarding, county shelter fees, spaying and neutering, Web site presence, equipment for special events, newsletter printing and distribution, etc. Fundraising professionals and savvy promoters are needed to plan and execute special events such as outdoor fairs, wine and cheese parties, themed dinners, silent auctions, eBay auctions, and sponsored athletic contests. Retail sales can include books, calendars, note cards, T-shirts, sweats, mugs, coasters, posters, artwork, agility equipment, etc. Other revenue options include the public supporters' use of affiliate credit cards and shopping with affiliate online retail companies. A percentage of the sales are donated to the rescue nonprofit.

The current economy has created a feeling of lack. Virtually all of the rescues are experiencing a loss of donations, as the number of dogs in need of rescue increases dramatically. If you do not have the time or the inclination to volunteer with a local organization, perhaps you will look into adoption, or make a donation to a rescue organization of your choice or from those featured here.

I have to confess that it wasn't until nine years ago that I became aware of this cause, after stumbling across a directory of animal rescue organizations. At that time I needed to overcome some nagging health problems and the loneliness of a divorce, so I placed a call to an organization in the Los Angeles area that specifically rescued golden retrievers (my favorite breed). They paired me up with a passionate young woman named Sara. Together we rescued purebred goldens and golden mixed breeds out of Ventura County's animal shelter, and often found them homes in the upscale communities of Thousand Oaks, Westlake, Ventura, and Santa Barbara. Sara and I worked as a "tag team" for a year, until she moved away and I needed a salaried job. My problems paled in comparison to the plight of these animals, and they helped me heal my life. Needless to say, it was by far the most positive and meaningful work that I've ever done, and the memories and images of those grateful dogs will remain with me forever.

It is my hope that you will enjoy the twenty-six short stories that represent some of the best canine rescue organizations throughout the state of California. They will make you laugh, cry, and celebrate the successful outcomes of rescued canines of many breeds. Please visit my Web site at http://www.doersofgood.com if you have a story that you would like to submit, as I'm looking for more heartwarming tales from rescue organizations in other states. I will leave you with these sobering statistics, which appear on the Web site of Animal Advocates Alliance, an editorial contributor to this book:

* Americans own 148 million dogs and cats. Only 18 percent are adopted from shelters.

* Six to eight million dogs and cats enter animal shelters. Half of them are euthanized.

* It is estimated that there are four thousand puppy mills operating in the United States. Up to four million puppy mill dogs are sold each year.

Thank you for purchasing *Rescued! Tales of California Canine Rescue.* You have now made a difference! Twenty percent of the profits from the sales from this book will be donated directly to the featured rescue organizations. Ponder and enjoy! Their stories are a cause of celebration!

Julie Anne Schubert

Abandoned in a Parking Lot

In April 2006, a brown and white, purebred English bulldog was abandoned in a busy shopping mall parking lot off of Route 15 in Victorville, on the way to Las Vegas. There he roamed the parking lot and dashed between cars in search of food, water, and shade. Luckily, the mall had a gas station and fast food restaurants. He was given handouts from passersby and restaurant workers but avoided human contact.

He must have been a scary sight to behold—a beast! Mange covered 80 percent of his body, in addition to blisters from the sun and heat. Calluses covered his elbows and knees. Long nails literally curled into the pads of his feet, making walking painful and difficult. There were warts on his face. The joints of his knees had a natural birth defect, and his eyes looked hazy from dry eye.

Two days passed and a Good Samaritan called animal control. Help arrived, and fate was on his side! He was taken to Riverside Animal Shelter, labeled as a "found stray," and his picture was posted on the Internet. Volunteers from the Southern California Bulldog Rescue (SCBR) monitored his posting, but no one showed up to claim or adopt him.

On the seventh and last day before being euthanized, Skip, the director of SCBR, called the shelter and asked that the bulldog be surrendered to them. Jackie, a volunteer, rescued him from the shelter and drove the exhausted bulldog to a waiting foster home. He had a good meal and rested there during the night. The next day he was taken to SCBR's preferred veterinarian, Dr. Roy.

Dr. Roy gave the dog the needed immunizations, medications for his severe skin infection, and drops for his dry eyes. His nails were clipped, and he had the first of many medicated baths to help heal his skin and restore his fur. The bulldog also had hip issues, and a burn mark around his neck was noted. He was severely malnourished, his skin paper-thin and fragile. Perhaps he spent years in a hot, dry, windy climate, which caused the eye problems. Perhaps he spent much of his time on concrete, which caused the calluses. Perhaps he was tethered by a rope, which caused the mark on his neck. He had so many issues for a dog so young. He was judged to be only five years old.

The bulldog spent a day at the veterinarian's office and was then driven to a new foster home with Skip in Santa Ana to begin many months in recovery. His new life with Southern California Bulldog Rescue began with a new name: "Tazz," from a cartoon character, the Tasmanian Devil. The name seemed appropriate for the bulldog with patches of fur and a tough spirit that had survived the worst of conditions. Tasmanian devils from Australia are stocky and muscular, not unlike stocky bulldogs that are sometimes described as fur-wrapped beer kegs with pushed-in faces! It is also said that bulldogs are like roses—you know one when you see one, and there are never two that look alike, just like humans! This was certainly true for this boy; he had his share of physical handicaps and deformities, which made him uniquely Tazz.

Now there was much healing to do in a loving foster home. His first week of recovery was mostly limited to sleeping in a separate room on his own, while his open skin lesions healed. From then on, he saw Dr. Roy twice a week for updates on his medications. His medical routine at home included the prescribed medicated baths, eye drops, and special medications for his skin.

Despite having a powerful name, Tazz was afraid of humans and other dogs and scampered away from meeting new guests. He spent hours outside hiding under shrubs, trying not to be noticed. He would eat and drink only when others were not in the room.

Days turned into weeks and weeks turned into months with Tazz making slow improvements and trusting those around him. He met other bulldogs that lived in his foster home. He took treats from a human hand. He learned to play with toys. He learned to enjoy the yard and lie in the grass. He learned to greet guests instead of running away when they arrived.

After six months, Tazz was a healthy, happy boy. He was well trained and his temperament was exceptional. In November and December, Tazz was adopted on a trial basis by two separate families, but he regressed to his timid nature. The adoptive families rejected him, citing his shyness, future medical expenses, and that he was unattractive.

Each time that Tazz returned home, he grew more dejected. The bulldog might have been unattractive, but he had a heart of gold. Skip was *not* going to put Tazz through yet another adoption process.

"Enough! Tazz is now mine!" Skip announced.

Tazz was officially adopted by Skip on January 7, 2007, and he loves his new family. He greets everyone at the front door with a happy dance and what Skip refers to as the "Tazz Tap" (the tap dance of his nails on the tile floor). He plays host to the foster dogs that stay awhile, and he's an inseparable buddy to Beau, another bulldog who is just over a year old. He loves his toys and shares them with Beau; they play together and have the run of the house. They even sleep together in Tazz's bed. But one of his favorite spots is laying in the middle of the deck at the hottest hour of the day; a habit from his previous life in the desert, perhaps?

Christmas is a special time of year at Skip's house. A "canine tree" is decorated with beautiful, handmade ornaments that depict each dog living in the house for that year. The ornaments have become family heirlooms, and they bring memories of their bulldogs that passed during the years and memories of the dogs that still remain with them. Tazz will have another ornament on the tree to commemorate another year, and Skip will once again celebrate a Christmas with the wonderful bulldog that no one wanted.

Southern California Bulldog Rescue (SCBR) was formed in 2004. They provide shelter, re-homing assistance, and funds for medical treatment for more than one hundred bulldogs each year. These dogs come from animal shelters, other rescue groups, and owners who wish to surrender their purebred bulldogs. SCBR helps bulldogs in Southern California find suitable homes. Their network consists of many volunteers who foster, do home checks, transport, and place bulldogs who come into the program. Over four hundred bulldogs have been placed through this organization during the last five years. Special events include the Bulldog Beauty Contest, Howl-o-ween, and Santa Paws. Other fundraising activities include eBay sales, calendar contests and sales, and joint activities with sister programs on the East Coast. SCBR's online store, featuring T-shirts, sweatshirts, hoodies, and accessories featuring their logo, is found at http://www.cafepress. com. Their newsletter, *Bullytin*, is available through e-mail. They rely entirely on donations for support. For more information, visit their Web site at http://www.socalbulldogrescue.org.

A Determined Dachshund Is Overcoming Paralysis

Author's Note: *Lee, Phillip, and Michele are three attorneys and the directors of Animal Advocates Alliance in Los Angeles. They work as a coordinated team for rescued dogs like Murphy.*

On Thursday, February 12, 2009, a two-year-old dachshund named Murphy was surrendered by its owner to the Baldwin Park Shelter in Los Angeles. Sadly, Murphy's back legs were paralyzed, and he was in pain from a problem in his spine. He had been suffering for quite some time.

By law, county shelters are obligated to euthanize an animal if it is experiencing "irremediable suffering." However, the shelter manager called Lee at Animal Advocates Alliance (AAA), and explained that he didn't want to put the dog down. Would Animal

Advocates Alliance be willing to rescue him ASAP? Lee agreed, grabbed her checkbook, left her office at 5:00 PM, and rushed through LA traffic to make the shelter closing time of 7:00 PM. When she spied Murphy, she knew that he was a special dog.

Lee related, "In spite of his pain, there was life in his eyes! If he could have wagged his tail, he would have! I put him in the seat next to me in the car, and he crawled over to lie in my lap as I was driving. I had tears in my eyes."

Lee met her boyfriend, Phillip, at a halfway point and handed Murphy over to him. Phillip drove Murphy to see Dr. Victor, AAA's veterinarian in Malibu, for evaluation. Dr. Victor kindly agreed to see the dog after closing time. The dog was in paralysis, and there was no time to lose.

X-rays showed a bulging disc that impinged on nerves in his spine. It was impossible to tell how long he'd been that way, and there was some concern that his paralysis was irreversible. However, Dr. Victor conducted some tests and found that there was some feeling in Murphy's back paws. He concluded that there was a chance of recovery and enough hope to proceed with surgery.

"Our response was to give him a best chance to walk again," Lee commented.

Friday was spent making telephone calls to various neurosurgeons in the Los Angeles area. The cost of the surgery was estimated to be ten thousand to twelve thousand dollars. They also told Lee that Murphy had a fifty–fifty chance at a full recovery. Unwavering, Lee pressed on and contacted the University of California at Davis, which is a veterinarian teaching school. Yes, they said they would be pleased to help Murphy for five thousand to six thousand dollars. Time was of the essence for a best outcome. Come ASAP, they said.

Michele contacted Dr. Victor, who again agreed to stay after hours to provide her with Murphy's health and vaccine certificates for surgery. Michele also made arrangements for Megan, an AAA volunteer, and Murphy to catch the last flight out of LAX on

Friday night. They boarded a plane at 10:30 PM and then spent the rest of the night at her sister's house in San Francisco. After a few hours of sleep, Megan and Murphy rose early and arrived at the UC Davis clinic at 6:00 AM for surgery on Saturday, February 14, Valentine's Day.

The surgery went well, the disc was repaired, and Murphy stayed to recover for two weeks. Then Lee flew up to Davis to pick him up and take him home—a forever home with her. Before boarding the plane, she carefully put him in a soft crate. There was a line of staples down his spine, which resembled a big zipper.

Murphy healed well, and after two to three weeks the staples were removed, and his fur grew back. Now the real work began for Murphy to walk again at a two-month rehabilitation program at the California Animal Rehabilitation Center in Santa Monica. Caring and encouraging staff members designed a special program that involved hydrotherapy, obstacle courses, and exercises. Murphy loved going, and AAA filmed his progress. At first he scooted around on his front legs, dragging his limp back legs behind him. But feeling in his hindquarters slowly returned, and they began teaching him to walk again.

His physical therapists suggested that in order to stabilize him and correct his posture, he needed a fitted wheelchair to support his back legs. AAA purchased a custom-designed cart from K-9 Carts. At first, he had trouble turning corners, but by the end of a week he was zipping around Lee's house at breakneck speed with pals Cleo and Newman, two sixty-pound rescued pit bulls.

Murphy's progress is remarkable. At the rehabilitation center, he is now standing on his back legs without the cart. It will take time to fully recover the ability to walk on his own, but he's making progress with the help of his physical therapist. They predict that he will make a full recovery.

In the meantime at home, the cart has been his joyful set of wheels. Murphy constantly rolls over Cleo's and Newman's paws and tails, as well as Lee's toes. Lee says that he zips around the house, stealing toys out of the pit bulls' mouths, which she finds hilarious. Lee, Phillip, Michele, Megan, and Murphy's doctors and physical therapists are very pleased with his progress. But most importantly, he has the rest of his life ahead of him—healed, whole, and complete.

Animal Advocates Alliance (AAA) was founded in 2008 and is dedicated to promoting the humane treatment of animals through legal advocacy, effecting social change through community education initiatives, and supporting of other animal rescue organizations. AAA rescues animals from city and county shelters, provides necessary veterinary care, and places the animals in safe and loving homes. Many of these animals have been neglected, suffered mental and/or physical abuse, or have physical injuries requiring surgery and rehabilitation.

AAA has their own community-based initiative aims to implement a program to schools, shelters, and adoptions events. They have also partnered up with Univision to air a weekly pet segment, and topics have included the importance of spaying/neutering, animal cruelty, and proper pet training. AAA works in tandem with other humane groups to promote spay/neuter education and to expose pet stores that sell animals from puppy mills. Most importantly, AAA engages in legal advocacy to support animal welfare legislation and facilitates aggressive prosecution of perpetrators of animal abuse under anticruelty statutes, including California Penal Code #597. As attorneys and animal advocates, they work pro bono with other organizations, such as the Best Friends Society, a large sanctuary in Utah whose volunteers transport rescued dogs from LA shelters to their facility. They also work with county agencies to set up mobile adoption units in parks during weekends, and to provide free spay/neuter services in South Los Angeles.

AAA effectively uses Facebook, Twitter, and a sophisticated Web site featuring videos to further their causes of animal rescue, adoption, and advocacy. AAA relies solely on donations from private donors, in-kind donations from local businesses, and the support of its dedicated volunteers. They greatly appreciate the generous contribution and continued assistance of their corporate partners and sponsors.

AAA features a store on their Web site offering pet apparel and gear, men's and women's apparel, mugs, cards, stickers, and more. For more information and to view a video about Murphy's rescue and rehabilitation, visit their Web site at http://www. animaladvocatesalliance.org.

Puppies! In a Dental Office???

In October 2002, a woman was at her wit's end. Her boyfriend abandoned a female pregnant dog in her back yard and tied it to a tree. She immediately called Animal Save, a rescue organization located in Grass Valley for help. Animal Save contacted the newly founded Pound Puppy Rescue, and the pregnant dog was rescued by Kathleen, the founder of this organization.

Daisy was a sweet, medium-sized "Heinz 57" dog with white, black, and brown fur, and she was due to have her puppies any day. Kathleen was pleased that Daisy and her puppies would soon be born in foster care, without the danger of them being exposed to illness and disease in a county shelter. Common problems for puppies in shelters are respiratory infections such as kennel cough, parvovirus, and distemper.

However, two challenges arose. Kathleen's husband, Russ, was not on board with fostering a pregnant dog. Thankfully, no excuses and asking for forgiveness allowed Daisy and the puppies a temporary home. The second challenge was that Kathleen had a full-time job in a dental office in Palo Alto. No excuses, she had to show up for work. Daisy could not be left alone during the day, so Kathleen fashioned a whelping box in her van: a children's plastic wading pool filled with fleece blankets. Problem solved. Daisy would go to work as well.

As the time approached for the puppies to arrive, Daisy was loveable, well-behaved, and absolutely devoted to her rescuer, Kathleen. Rescue dogs always seem incredibly grateful and bond quickly with their new family. Daisy bonded by sleeping on the bed, snuggled between Kathleen and her husband.

One night before falling asleep, Kathleen pleaded, "Daisy, please don't have your puppies tonight. I need my sleep! And please, no more than six because I don't think that I can handle more than that."

One morning, a week after Daisy's rescue, Kathleen prepared to go to work. She carefully loaded the very pregnant girl into the whelping box in the back of the van and left for work. Within minutes, Daisy began to pant and jump the seats, landing in Kathleen's lap.

"Daisy, you can't have your puppies now! Please wait until we get there."

Kathleen soon arrived at the dental office and parked the van under a window of the building, where she and her coworkers could keep an eye on her. Then she tucked Daisy back into her whelping box, offering encouragements.

"Listen, I'm going into the office, and I'm going to leave you here for now. I promise to check on you. Good girl, I know that you can do it!"

Kathleen and her coworkers Cecilia and Claudia made quick dashes outside to check on her. The first puppy arrived at 9:00 AM, and the second thirty minutes later. By 12:30, no more puppies had been born. Kathleen and her coworkers were concerned. Finally, the third puppy was born, but it was stillborn. It was a chilly day, and Kathleen, Cecilia, and Claudia made the decision to bring Daisy and the puppies inside for warmth. They smuggled the dogs into the dental office, into the employee break room!

The women continued to check, and by 5:00 PM, Daisy had a total of eight puppies, four of them born in the dental office that afternoon. Two were stillborn, but six were alive and doing well. During the excitement, Dr. Greg stumbled upon the break room occupants, but just shrugged his shoulders and wished Kathleen good luck.

That evening at home before bedtime, Daisy was taken outside to relieve herself. She and her six adorable puppies then retired to their whelping box for the night. Early the next morning, Kathleen prepared for work and carefully placed the puppies in a big basket and walked Mommy Daisy to the van.

"Daisy, your puppies are so cute! One, two, three, four, five, six ... *seven*??"

Daisy had delivered another puppy that first evening when no one was watching!

As the weeks went by, Daisy slept with Kathleen and Russ on the bed and would sneak back to nurse her babies at intervals during the night. During weekdays, Daisy and the puppies commuted to work with Kathleen with Dr. Greg's blessing. Once the puppies opened their eyes and were able to walk around, a pen was put on a patio underneath a tree, where neighbors and patients socialized with them and got their "puppy fix." It was a win–win for everyone.

The puppies actually became Dr. Greg's therapy dogs. His patients held the puppies while he drilled their teeth! And children who were patients of Dr. Greg loved going to the dentist. Dr. Greg soon became known as the "Palo Alto dentist with the puppies." Many litters and mama dogs came to the office during the course of seven years.

All of Daisy's puppies found good homes. It was a long wait, but Daisy found her "forever" home, too. She now lives with Noah and Kelly in a home in Oakland. They adore her. She is totally a spoiled girl, and at night she sleeps with them under the covers.

Pound Puppy Rescue was founded in 2001, and is comprised of twenty-five volunteers who rescue more than two hundred puppies every year. Their mission is to keep the dogs out of overcrowded shelters, where they are at risk for disease and euthanasia. Pregnant dogs, nursing dogs, and puppies are mainly rescued from shelters and other canine rescue organizations unequipped to handle them. The puppies are placed into foster homes, where they are kept healthy, socialized, and in their litter until they are old enough to be placed in permanent, loving homes. Activities are centered in the San Francisco Bay Area, but rescues have spanned as far north as Eureka and south to the Central Valley, including Bakersfield. For more information, visit their Web site at http://www.poundpuppyrescue.org.

Four Female Angels Rescue Injured Brennen

A black, tri-colored, purebred Australian shepherd helplessly found himself in the Los Angeles North Central Animal Care Shelter with two broken legs and an abrasion on his head. Little did he know that four female "angel" volunteers would spring into action to save his life and create for him a new, healthy, and happy one.

A most important player in rescue, a shelter employee, took the shepherd's picture and posted it on the Internet. There was no time to waste, as injured dogs are routinely scheduled for euthanasia.

Diane from Aussie Rescue So Cal saw the posting and quickly drove down to LA's North Central shelter and paid the adoption fee. Shelter workers helped her carry the forty-five-pound male to her car and gently placed him in a blanketed back seat. Diane said, "He was alert, smiling, and wagging his tail! I intuited that this rescued dog was special and named him Brennen after my good friend, Doreen."

Doreen Brennen had recently died of cancer and bequeathed money to the organization for an injured dog to make a full and complete recovery. And thanks to a match made by a woman named Chris at the generous Hogan Foundation, Brennen's orthopedic surgeon's bill of six thousand dollars was paid for.

Now the real healing began with a new woman by the name of Becky. Her specialty is fostering injured dogs through lengthy rehabilitation. She guessed Brennen to be two years old or less, and with a puppy personality, being confined to a crate for over three months would be a real challenge, long and tedious. But she was his new mommy, and it was time to get creative and fun.

Becky related her secrets: "The trick was to keep Brennen's environment in his crate stimulating for him. His wrists were broken, and standing was impossible at first. I took him outside eight times a day to enjoy fresh air and to relieve himself with the help of a flannel-lined sling. I also placed his crate in an entryway of the house, so he almost always had sight of me and our other dogs in the great room and first floor of the house. He needed to feel included with our activities. Brennen spent time outside every day, so he could watch the birds and squirrels."

She continued. "Nearly every day I read him stories from *Bark Magazine* and *Whole Dog Journal*, put the television on the Animal Planet channel for Brennen to watch, and played funny little games with him. His favorite was 'find the treats under the paper cups.' He loved to be brushed and pampered. Keeping him occupied with food and treats kept him busy. His 'happy meals' consisted of low-fat and high-protein treats, frozen yogurt for dogs from an opened cardboard cup, a kong filled with kibble and canned food, and marrow bones.

"Nearly every dog confined to a crate must have no more than three small meals a day. The rule is that they must not gain weight, so that it makes it easier to rebound on mended bones."

At the end of the recovery period, Becky s-l-o-w-l-y walked him around the property and worked with him in the backyard pool doing water therapy. His life vest had a zipper along the back with a handle, and she guided him around her in small circles. She did this for three weeks, until his legs were strong again.

Today, Brennen is happy and healthy in his forever home with Jill and Jeff in San Diego. They have no children, if you're not counting Brennen. His job is in service to Jill, to guard and entertain her during the day in her office at home. If Brennen could talk, he would thank his four female rescue angels, Diane, Doreen, Chris, and Becky, for his new life.

Aussie Rescue So Cal consists of approximately six part-time volunteers and five foster families who rescue and temporarily foster dogs at risk from city and county shelters. Their territory usually consists of the counties of Los Angeles, San Bernardino, Riverside, San Diego, Orange, and the Central Coast. Three dogs were recently rescued from Kern County. In addition, their Web site provides the public extraordinary access to a multitude of county shelters and other Aussie rescue organizations through links. Fundraising activities include online solicitations for dogs with specific medical needs and occasional appearances at pet fairs. Donations directly impact the number of animals that can be rescued and cared for. In a good year, as many as fifty dogs are rescued and found forever homes. For more information, visit http://www.aussierescuesocal.com.

Jake Successfully Competes with Human World-Class Athletes

In 2002, a year-old, handsome, purebred golden retriever was sprung from a Los Angeles county shelter by a volunteer from Golden Retriever Rescue of Greater LA. He weighed only fifty-six pounds, but a rugged, 6'5" swimmer named Jeff from San Diego saw potential, and he wanted a companion.

Jeff first taught Jake to swim in a pool and to be comfortable and relaxed in the water. Upon doing this, Jeff noticed that Jake's back legs were not kicking properly. Using a ball as an incentive to fetch, Jake eventually learned to move and kick with all of his legs to be an efficient swimmer.

Jake easily took to ocean swimming. To build endurance, his land exercise consisted of sprints on the beach and tennis ball retrieval. Jeff gradually got Jake to swim around ocean buoys in La Jolla for two miles, twice a week. At that time, Jeff was training to swim the English Channel.

In 2004, Jeff realized that his goal to swim the English Channel was not going to happen, but another perilous swim of 1.5 miles with strong currents and cold water beckoned for both of them: Alcatraz. The Alcatraz Invitational swim is held annually by the South End Rowing Club, whose members consist of judges, lawyers, and congressmen. They were surprised when Jeff submitted an application for his dog. Members of the club were skeptical that a dog could swim that far.

But Jeff successfully made his case, and the two athletes headed north to San Francisco on July 29, 2005. They stayed at the Hyatt, and with conspiratorial help from the staff, Jake and Jeff rode the glass elevator up to their room and then went out for a late-night walk. The next day breakfast was delivered by room service, and Jake's protein meal was scrambled eggs.

They were ferried out with approximately five hundred other swimmers. As VIPs, they sat on the top deck next to the press. Jeff and Jake were the first to go, and the captain announced to all on the boat: "Ladies and gentlemen, Jake the Dog will lead the swim this year!" The two athletes paraded down amid the clapping and shouting swimmers to a wood plank, six feet up from the water. Jeff jumped in first and called to Jake. Jake hesitated, but once the dog was in the choppy water, he swam over to Jeff.

The two of them took off with a slight lead from the other swimmers. Jeff swam behind him, and occasionally touched Jake's back feet to let him know that he was right behind. At two hundred yards, seven professional athletes caught up with them and passed them like a pack of racehorses. Wanting to catch up, Jake took off after them.

Jeff knew that the dog would burn out too soon if left to his own devices, and from time to time, he pulled the dog backward by his hind legs to slow him down. Then Jake got tired and Jeff changed tactics. To find Jake that extra energy needed to finish the race, he swam with him, side by side, yelling encouragements: "Go get the ball!" "You can do it!" "Good boy, keep going!!"

Jake dog-paddled his way into history at the shoreline next to the Hyde Street Pier in forty-one minutes and forty-five seconds. He came in seventy-second and Jeff seventy-third out of more than five hundred swimmers. To Jeff's surprise, there was a crowd of people on shore waiting for them and chanting, "Jake! Jake! Jake!" After the dog left the water, the crowd cheered and the media captured his finish. Tail wagging, he trotted past a woman who tried to put a medal around his neck. He appeared on every national television news channel, including CNN, and around the world on the Internet.

Swimming San Francisco Bay is difficult. There are strong currents, and the salt water is frigid and rough. Swimmers must leave at the perfect time of day and aim for an exact destination or they will be taken down by the currents. Jake might have stolen the show, but it was Jeff and Jake who conquered the challenge together as a team.

Jake is now eight years old and is in such great shape that Jeff believes that he could still make that swim. In fact, he swims long distances in the ocean nearly every day, and people cannot believe what he does. It is an epic story and a fateful one, considering the fact that seven years ago he was found in a shelter and easily scaled a seven-foot fence! To view Jake online, visit http://www.jaketheswimmingdog.com.

Golden Retriever Club of Greater Los Angeles Rescue, Inc. (GRCGLAR) was founded in 2001 but was an informal operation for many years through their parent breed club. They have the distinction of being the oldest golden retriever rescue organization in continuous operation in Southern California. In 2006, this organization ranked among the three largest golden retriever rescues in the United States. GRCGLAR has a 130-member, all-volunteer force operating in six counties, and have taken in over 3,200 goldens since 2003. Although they stand ready to help any golden retriever in need, their commitment to the neediest cases, the old, the sick, and the injured, remains unparalleled in the rescue community. All monies go directly toward the care and placement of their rescue dogs from Southern California. Ongoing partnered activities outside of California include Project Taiwan and the Gold Rush Puppy Mill Rescue in Oklahoma. Project Taiwan has brought home approximately fifty healthy and rehabilitated goldens since January 2009.

GRCGLAR conducts annual special events, such as the Holiday eBay Auction, the Dogtoberfest annual reunion, and the Fields of Gold Calendar Drive. Other fundraising activities include memorial donations and gift cards, monthly pledges called the Shamrock Circle Fund, online shopping, the Golden Galleria and Bookstore on their Web site, eBay auctions, daily donation programs, and various community programs. Cause-related marketing partnerships with businesses, philanthropists, and individuals are encouraged. All support through tax-deductible donations and participation in creative marketing partnerships and community programs is greatly appreciated! For more information, visit http://www.grcglarescue.org.

All Is Well with Gucci

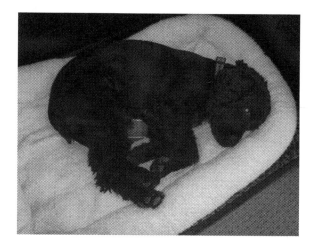

Rick and his partner Ron have always taken in dogs that needed homes. In September of 2002, they filled out adoption forms with Emily from Living Is for Everyone (LIFE) based in Agoura, California. It was love at first sight and a fast adoption with a blonde-and-white cocker spaniel that they named Coco. A few months later they found Coco a black-and-white "parti" cocker companion from a rescue organization in San Diego. They promptly named her Chanel. Chanel had been terribly abused, but they gave her a wonderful, pampered life for seven years until she died suddenly from a liver disease in the summer of 2009.

Coincidentally, Emily from LIFE was summoned by a volunteer at the Camarillo shelter to come and rescue a black female cocker spaniel. She was in bad shape and very frightened. She stood no chance of surviving the shelter without intervention from a rescue organization. LIFE sprang into action: a veterinarian tended to an abscess in her neck and spayed her, and a groomer worked on her dirty, badly matted coat.

A week went by as the cocker mended from the surgery. It was now Saturday, the day of every week that the rescue featured their fostered dogs at PetSmart in Westlake Village. Emily and her volunteers debated whether they should take their new girl. She still had a drain in her neck from the recent surgery, and did not look presentable for adoption. But at the last minute they changed their minds and packed her up as well.

As luck would have it, Rick planned a trip to PetSmart that morning to replace a broken water bowl for Coco. He wanted a specially designed bowl for cocker spaniels with long ears, and PetSmart sold them. As he approached the entrance to the store, he spied Emily and the LIFE dogs available for adoption.

It had been seven years since Rick and Ron had successfully adopted Coco from Emily, yet he remembered her. He scanned the many fostered dogs and spied the poor, black cocker with the drain in her neck. Without a word, he hurried home to tell Rick about the female cocker that was healing from surgery. It was a no-brainer. As they left their house, Ron said to Rick, "Let's name her Gucci or Prada."

The men returned with a leash. As Emily, Rick, and Ron were signing the adoption documents and chatting with Emily, she casually added, "By the way, our records show that your dog's name is Gucci."

Rick and Ron went numb. "We were absolutely shocked!" they reported. "We *all* had goose bumps! It's hard to believe, isn't it? She was absolutely meant for us, and we for her. I showed up at Pet Smart on the right day, at the right time for what I thought was an errand to buy a water dish. Go figure!"

The three-year-old Gucci is now a great companion to the ten-year-old Coco. Together they make good company for Rick, a retired advertising executive. They routinely see a groomer, play with tennis balls, and go to lunch at an outdoor café in Westlake

Village. Vacations are spent in Palm Springs. And both of them have personalized designer water bowls from PetSmart!

Living Is for Everyone (LIFE) began in 1992 by a seventeen-year-old woman, devastated by the tragic loss of her dog, Alfie. She decided to forego college and put her time and energy into saving the lives of local animals at risk. Since then, the LIFE animal rescue organization has saved over eight thousand animals, 90 percent of them from county shelters. The organization operates on a fourteen-acre property, where family members and volunteers care for fostered animals in comfortable home settings. Their mission is to rescue homeless or abandoned dogs and cats and place them into permanent, responsible, and loving homes. LIFE promotes and practices an aggressive spay/neuter effort to help resolve the pet overpopulation problem. They are an all-volunteer organization, relying solely on donations to continue the work. Fundraising activities include a casino night and a yearly newsletter. For more information, visit their Web site at http://www.lifeanimalrescue.org.

Lucy and Ricky Survive "Nowhere Ville"

Author's Note: *Spouses of canine rescue volunteers unwittingly find themselves involved with rescues. This is the story of a construction worker, tired from a day's work, who was alert to a tragic situation. He stopped and did the right thing, as did Southern California Labrador Retriever Rescue, by coming to the aid of dogs that were not clearly "of breed."*

On March 21, 2008, it was a Friday afternoon around 4:00 PM. Steve had finished a full week of building construction work and was headed home for cold soda and air conditioning. He was only fifteen minutes from home at 175th Street East and Pear Blossom Highway, a remote, desolate corner between Victorville and Palmdale, home to an old, vacant gas station. It was "Nowhere

Ville," where humans didn't venture out much. He spied a pair of dogs in an open pen. He had never noticed them before.

Something is not right, he thought.

Steve turned around and headed back to investigate, parking near a couple of other men who had also stopped to investigate. One was a highway patrol officer. They saw a pair of thin but handsome golden retrievers trapped inside a makeshift pen of flimsy wire that had been constructed on an old pad of concrete. Worse, there was no water, no food, no shade, and the temperature was nearly one hundred degrees. The dogs appeared to be a mother and son, and her son looked to be less than a year old. Sadly, he had a heavy gauge wire tightly wrapped around his neck. Both dogs were wagging their tails! Help had arrived!

The three men discussed their options. With no collars and no identification, the dogs were freed. The officer offered to take one dog home, but Steve spoke up. "My wife is a member of Labrador Retriever Rescue, and her organization will find them great homes. Please, let me take both of them home, and she will get them medical care; they may be dehydrated and sick."

The men agreed, and Steve carefully loaded the happy retrievers into the passenger seat of his pick-up truck. It was almost his wife Jennifer's birthday, and he knew that she would be pleased. He turned on the air conditioner and quickly headed home.

Jennifer and Steve named the pair Lucy and Ricky, and Steve removed the wire that was tightly wrapped around Ricky's neck. Lucy was in the worst physical shape and had a bad skin condition from malnutrition. Jennifer spent days tending to Lucy. Luckily, there were no broken bones or serious injuries and they soon went into new homes for temporary foster care. Lucy was judged to be two years old and her son, Ricky, was still a young pup at approximately eight months.

In rescue, there seems to be a universal law that the dogs who experience the worst of conditions will wind up in new homes under the best of conditions. Lucy was adopted by Kim, who nursed her through a difficult spay surgery and depression from trauma. Now as Bodhi (meaning "enlightened being" in Sanskrit), she is truly happy and healthy, weighing sixty-five pounds. Kim calls her "a *very* special dog," and she's a companion to a black lab and two cats. Bodhi spends many hours hiking the Santa Monica Mountains with Kim and Gidget, her best buddy, and romping on the beaches of Malibu.

Ricky, now seventy-three pounds, was adopted by Steve from Hermosa Beach. He is loved by a family of four and is exceptionally intelligent, loving, and mindful of personal relationships within the family and friends. He sleeps with the thirteen-year-old son, and then slips upstairs to sleep next to Steve, who calls the dog "a blessing to our family." He can be found taking long walks along the Strand.

Southern California Labrador Retriever Rescue, Inc. (SCLRR) was founded in 1998, and is currently comprised of over one hundred volunteers dedicated to assisting Labrador retrievers in need. All funds go toward their mission of rehabilitating, re-homing, and educating the public about these wonderful dogs. Current area coverage consists of the following counties: Los Angeles, Orange, Ventura, and Santa Barbara. Victorville and surrounding areas are covered on a very limited basis. (SCLRR does not operate in the counties of San Diego, Riverside, or San Bernardino.) General donations pay for shelter fees, vaccinations, spaying and neutering, equipment for events, and newsletter distribution. Their yearly newsletter, *Highlights*, is available online as well. The Polly Memorial Fund is reserved for emergencies of their fostered dogs, and the Senior Labrador Rescue Program provides financial support for the medical needs and boarding that seniors often require. For more information, including special events, visit their Web site at http://www.sclrr.org, and http://www.sclrr.org/calendar.cgi.

One-eyed Man Adopts a One-eyed Dog

Author's Note: *Before Save Animals from Euthanasia (SAFE) became a nonprofit organization, two sisters, Kelli in Thousand Oaks and Susan in Santa Clarita, rescued sick and injured dogs from the medical and veterinarian wards of county shelters. They found these dogs proper veterinarian care, nursed them back to health, and carefully placed them with suitable owners. This memorable story is one that unfolded for Kelli in 2007, the year that the sisters came to the aid of fifty dogs.*

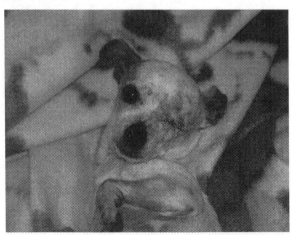

The white-and-cream male Chihuahua weighed only six or seven pounds. It was well below normal weight and estimated to be approximately four years old. Someone dropped him off at an emergency veterinarian's office in Ventura and quickly left: no tags, no information, no explanation.

The doctor kindly tended to the injured dog. His left eye was removed and stitched shut, and his twisted leg was put in a cloth sling to keep it stable. Unable to keep him, the veterinarian instructed an office assistant to drive the dog to the Ventura County Animal Shelter in Camarillo, California, where he would be available for adoption. The shelter volunteers cared for him and affectionately named him Stitch.

Injured dogs who find themselves at a county shelter stand little chance of being adopted, unless it is by a rescue organization. Fortunately for Stitch, luck was on his side. Kelli spied the tiny, one-eyed Chihuahua in the medical building, scooped him up, and took him home. He was crated for six weeks, as his injured leg needed time to heal. There he assimilated into her home as a foster dog with her own two: Lola, a Yorkshire terrier, and Loco, a female Chihuahua.

How am I going to find you a good home, Stitch? Kelli wondered. *It's out there, little one. I'll find it for you … somehow.*

She regularly brought her dogs to a local dog park for exercise and socialization, as Stitch remained in his crate. One day, a middle-aged man carefully watched them, and finally approached the dog crate and looked inside. To his surprise, a one-eyed dog stared back at him.

He identified himself as Glenn, also a resident of Thousand Oaks. Then Glenn introduced her to his eleven-year-old Chihuahua named Chiquita (she had been his mother's), as well as a younger Chihuahua–dachshund mix named Rufus.

Glenn continued. "How much do you want for him?"

"One hundred and twenty dollars."

"I don't have that much. I'm blind in my left eye, too. I figure that this dog and I need to stick together!"

The conversation continued, and Kelli was touched by the man's sincerity. He was a kindred soul to Stitch! An intuitive feeling came over Kelli. He could be a great match for the Chihuahua, but she needed more information. She took the man's contact information and promised to call for a house check.

The house check confirmed her intuitive feeling. He lived by himself in a home that he inherited from his mother and got by on a fixed disability income. His dogs were his life, and he provided them with a comfortable, loving, and happy home.

Glenn was allowed to adopt Stitch without paying an adoption fee. Today, Stitch is called Willy (for One-eyed Willy), and he lives happily ever after with Glenn, Chiquita, and Rufus. Kelli pays Glenn's veterinarian bills; not that he's ever asked her to.

Save Animals from Euthanasia (SAFE) was formed in 2007 and is dedicated to rescuing the sick, injured, overlooked, and forgotten small dogs due to their medical condition. They have successfully rehabilitated and placed dogs with mange, eye removal, leg amputation, skin conditions, tumors, broken bones, spinal injuries, cherry eye, head trauma, and otherwise "unadoptable" problems. SAFE operates with a core of four rescue volunteers and ten foster volunteers. Their dogs are regularly seen on Saturdays at a PETCO with yellow or orange "Adopt Me" vests. However, many of the adoptions actually occur throughout the week in a local dog park! One hundred percent of all donations go directly to the care of the animals. Any amount donated is greatly appreciated and helps the workers care for those dogs that deserve a chance for a happy life. For more information, visit their Web site at http://www.safeanimalrescue.org.

Born to Be Wild in Sacramento

Exactly one month after the passing of a special family dog, a family from Hidden Valley in Northern California was destined to find another. The family of four was in mourning after the passing of their family dog, Sadie, in January 2006.

"I need a dog today," texted Tyler, the eleven-year-old older son of Karin and Terry. The family was in San Francisco walking along a path near the bay toward the SPCA. Tyler had gone on ahead and was thinking about his need for a new buddy.

"I know, honey. I'm looking," replied Karin.

Karin had spent the past several weeks looking online for a mature dog at rescue Web sites, local or not local, that would fit the family's needs: a buddy and companion for Tyler and a playmate and guardian for four-year-old Konner. A few opportunities fell through, but Karin persisted.

The morning of the text message, approximately one month to the day after they lost Sadie, Karin saw a picture and read the description of a chocolate Labrador retriever named Coco. The five-year-old girl was available at an adoption event in Folsom that very day. Staring at Coco's picture, Karin had a strong, intuitive feeling that Coco was the dog that they had been looking for.

Karin, Terry, and Konner hurriedly left to make the event in Folsom by 1:00 PM, which was three hours away. They arrived at 12:15. Terry was busy getting Konner out of the car when Karin spied Coco. There was another family inspecting her, and Karin was nervous. She brazenly pushed her way forward to the dog and picked up Coco's leash. A surprised rescue volunteer walked up to Karin.

Karin said, "I'm *very* interested in this dog. We drove three hours to get here to see her today. My husband and son will be here shortly. May I take her for a walk?"

The volunteer obliged. Coco was polite, curious, and alert and exuded a positive personality. Terry went to get the checkbook as Karin asked for adoption paperwork and answered questions from the volunteer, who recognized that a bond had already developed between them.

Coco had been an owner-surrendered dog, and she had stayed at the SPCA and Central California Lab rescue for some time. Now she would be going home with a family who needed her: a four-year-old with a full-time babysitter and an eleven-year-old boy. She would have a big, fenced-in back yard, a doggy door, and her own bed. Coco happily got into their minivan, which was nearly identical to her foster mom's minivan. They drove straight to pick up Tyler, and then on to Karin's parents' house to introduce the Lab to her new extended family. The family decided to name the new dog Coco Elizabeth, after Karin's grandmother, Elizabeth, who had recently passed on. Karin had promised her grandmother that if she had a daughter, she would name her Elizabeth, and the female dog would be treated as such.

Fast forward to nine months later. It was December 24, Christmas Eve, and Karin, Terry, Konner, and Coco Elizabeth traveled to Sacramento for a five-hour consultation and evaluation by doctors at the MIND Institute (Medical Investigation of Neural/Developmental Disorders), regarding Konner's developmental difficulties. Coco remained in the car as the doctors confirmed a diagnosis of autism, which had been suspected over the years but not confirmed. They then drove to the Doubletree Hotel in downtown Sacramento, where they had reservations to stay that evening. They smuggled the Lab into their hotel suite, as dogs were not allowed.

It had been a tedious and trying day for everyone. Konner and Coco watched television in the living room of the suite, as Karin made emotional telephone calls to family members and friends in the next room. Terry decided to duck across the street to a large shopping mall to buy a few last-minute gifts.

Several phone calls later, Karin realized that things were too quiet in the living room. She checked to find that Konner and Coco were gone! A mother's worst nightmare: a four-year-old who wanders and hides with a dog not on a leash in a sprawling hotel on twenty acres. The three-storied building had hallways like spokes of a wheel containing 450 rooms, fronting onto a busy boulevard. Luckily, Konner was wearing an ID bracelet that read: "autism disorder—speech delayed—allergic to wheat and dairy," as well as his name, date of birth, and three cell phone numbers. Coco was wearing her collar with proper ID as well. Karin immediately alerted the front desk and security and explained that the nonverbal child was wearing a bracelet, he could be acting strangely or hiding, and the dog was friendly.

"Is there any chance he would have no pants on?" the front desk replied.

"Well, yes, he likes to take them off, and he's wearing a T-shirt that says 'Born to be Wild'."

"Would he have a dog with him? A big, brown dog was seen with him in the lobby."

"Ah, yes."

Karin sighed. Coco was guarding him.

From then on, it was all hands on deck. The manager ran through the hotel, coordinating the search. Every employee available was called as a search team and scoured the elevators, common areas, hallways, and rooms, communicating with walkie-talkies. Karin went downstairs and frantically asked guests if they had seen the pair. Yes, they were reported to have been in elevators and hallways—always on the move.

A short time later, there was a shout from the manager. The child and dog were found in an upstairs third-floor hallway, outside of a room directly above theirs on the second floor. Evidently, Konner and the dog traveled in the elevator and got off on the wrong floor, which looked identical to theirs. Using her superior instincts and memory of direction, Coco Elizabeth guided Konner to what she thought was his hotel room. Then she herded him into an alcove, not letting him leave. Coco was found exhausted and stressed by the ordeal. Konner showed his rescuers his ID bracelet, which Karin had coached him to do if he got lost.

Everyone agreed that Coco Elizabeth faithfully assumed and carried out her duties as guardian and protector of her four-year-old boy. Who knows, maybe she had some help from Grandmother Elizabeth watching from Heaven!

Now Konner is eight years old and attends the second grade. He has a one-on-one aide and receives speech and occupational therapy. His sister, Coco Elizabeth, is treated like a queen and sleeps in her Tempur-Pedic bed under her purple, velvet blanket.

Central California Labrador Retriever Rescue (CCLRR) was founded in 1998 to answer the need to find loving homes for abused, abandoned, or unwanted Labrador retrievers in the Central Valley. This organization of approximately twenty volunteers covers Greater Sacramento south to Merced. Their Central Valley chapter was needed to counter the tremendous pet overpopulation in Fresno County, and adoption events are held in Fresno every month, thanks to cooperation of the River Park Management. CCLRR routinely rescues and places approximately four hundred Labs every year into loving homes. Special events include Big Hat Days and Clovis Fest. Fundraising activities include partners such as Jamba Juice, Rubio's, and Macy's Shop for a Cause. For more information, visit http://www.cc-labrescue.org and http://www.cclabrescuecvc.org.

Veterinary Care for Nevada County Animals: Bandit's Story

In August 2009, a young boxer with a crooked smile was found in a rural community called Penn Valley. He was horribly emaciated and resting on the property of a man who took him to his local county shelter for help.

The Nevada County Animal Shelter has one of the most rehabilitative programs in the United States, thanks to Sammie's

Friends, a nonprofit organization dedicated to paying for diagnosis, treatment, surgery, and rehabilitation for virtually all of its animal occupants, as well as other animals who need help in Nevada County.

The boxer was very frail, weighing only twenty-six pounds, and estimated to be two years old. Cheryl from Sammie's Friends named him Bandit and sprang into action. Tests were needed to determine why he could barely eat and eliminate his food. After two veterinarian specialists could not find the cause of the problem with blood tests, ultra sounds, and needle aspirants, a third local doctor, Dr. Tim, suggested exploratory surgery. This option was deemed the most risky due to the boxer's weakened condition. Cheryl decided to take a chance, as he would surely die in a matter of days.

Dr. Tim did indeed find the problem: a large tumor blocking the entrance to his intestines. It was thought that the tumor was caused by an ulcer, which was probably caused by ingesting a foreign object. He proceeded with the surgery, and then their worst fears came to pass. Bandit died on the operating table.

Suesan, Dr. Tim's technical assistant, gave him oxygen but to no avail. She then gave him mouth-to-mouth respiration, and miraculously, he came back to life and began breathing on his own. With the tumor removed, Bandit was stitched up and placed in a kennel for recovery.

The clinic closed in the evenings, which presented a problem for Bandit. Suesan kindly took the dog home with her, so she could keep a watchful eye on him through the night and administer pain killers and first aid, if needed. It was that night that he actually was able to drink liquid food called Nutra Cal, and she slept with him in a spare room of her house.

Suesan and her entire family cared for Bandit for three weeks. Her daughter, son, and husband also slept in the spare room with the dog, rotating night by night. Bonnie, a friend who lived nearby, cared for Bandit some days while Suesan and her family were away.

With the tumor removed, Bandit began to gain weight and was expected to make a full recovery and live a long, healthy life. He was given prescribed pureed canned food, and he ate small amounts three to five times a day. He hungrily wolfed down as much food as his system allowed, as if making up for all that time that he couldn't eat. In the meantime, kind donors who had learned about Bandit through the Sammie's Friends Web site sent funds to pay the medical bills, which eventually totaled three thousand dollars. In September, Bandit went to live in his forever home in Half Moon Bay, across the street from the beach, with Cameo, his buddy, a pit bull/Labrador mixed breed, two rat terriers, and three cats.

Here is what his new family recently said about Bandit: "He weighs about forty-five pounds now. The weight gain is slowing. He eats three times a day. You can still see his ribs, but not like before. The area on his back between his hips and chest has doubled! He's gaining a lot of strength, too. He pulls a lot on his walks and is afraid of *nothing*. He pulls towards people, dogs, cars, and the garbage truck by standing on his hind legs and leaning forward. Bandit needs to be on leash most of the time. He's becoming strong by playing with Cameo. He runs faster than the wind, and his game is 'chase me if you can.' It is like he's living the puppyhood he missed; he's curious, innocent, energetic, playful, and mischievous all at the same time! Bandit is well socialized and plays with other dogs in the neighborhood and dog park. He's been seen running carefree in the hills of San Gregorio overlooking the ocean. And when he sleeps, his long tongue sticks out the side of his crooked smile."

The adoption of Bandit by Loren and Lydia was bittersweet for Suesan. She continues her important work as a vet tech at Mother Lode Veterinary Hospital in Grass Valley. She has a deep passion for animals, owning three dogs, six cats, and a horse.

Suesan remarked, "Helping animals is like a ministry to me. I'm proud to be a part of the board of Sammie's Friends."

Sammie's Friends (SF) was founded in 2004. They are dedicated to providing the medical care for the animals at the Nevada County Animal Shelter, making them adoptable, and to support other disadvantaged animals in Nevada County that, without help, would be placed in the shelter or euthanized. SF pays for diagnostic costs, surgery, and rehabilitation so that these animals may go on to lead happy, healthy lives in forever homes.

The euthanasia rate at Nevada County's shelter was at 68 percent. Thanks to the vision of Sheryl Wicks and one hundred volunteers, plus the nonprofit organization called Sammie's Friends and an adoption Web site by Dawn Allmandinger, the euthanasia rate is now 2 percent. The shelter's dogs have found homes in the Bay Area and other parts of California, Illinois, Indiana, Idaho, Texas, Arizona, Utah, Nevada, Washington, Montana, Minnesota, Oregon, Colorado, and British Columbia. This massive volunteer effort and grassroots organization has been credited for saving approximately eight thousand dogs and cats since 2004, and approximately 450 dogs in 2009.

SF consists of volunteers who write grants, exercise dogs at the shelter, and plan and execute public relations and special events. There is no foster program, as the Nevada County shelter is used to temporarily house the animals until adoption. Fundraising consists of local community events, public relations, and obtaining grants. A quarterly newsletter called *The Poop Scoop* is available online and through e-mail. For more information, visit http://www.sammiesfriends.org.

Action Jackson Becomes a Star of Extreme Stunts

In 2006, a handsome, white-and-brown Jack Russell terrier named Rusty was abandoned and placed in a Los Angeles County Shelter. When Eldad from the Hope for Paws animal rescue organization found him, he was sick from kennel cough, a respiratory virus common to shelters. He was so dejected that he wouldn't raise his head to acknowledge the people who came to his cage. Eldad had never seen a dog so miserable, so he rescued him on the spot and brought him home.

From the beginning it was obvious that his previous owners abused him. He cowered whenever an object was picked up, and he wanted to be left alone. However, in just two days, Eldad and his wife, Audrey, perked him up, and he began to feel better.

In fact, it was revealed that he had an obsession—with playing ball!

It was not known whether Rusty ever played with a tennis ball, but he developed an insatiable appetite for fetching one for hours! All he wanted to do was have Eldad or Audrey toss out the ball for him to catch, over and over and over. He was fast, and if they did not immediately throw it, he would bark at them to hurry up. He chased every ball that anyone threw, stole other dogs' balls, and dropped those balls at strangers' feet to play. He was driven! One day he played so long that when they returned home, they noticed blood on the floor. Rusty's paws were torn and bleeding, which *still* did not preclude the little dog from wanting to fetch the ball.

The couple was at their wit's end with Rusty's behavior when one day they got a call from a famous trainer for stunt dogs. He was looking for a dog with speed and athletic agility to perform at large venues such as sporting events, theme parks, expos, and state and county fairs, aimed at teaching people the amazing talents of dogs. He explained that his entire troupe of canine stars came from rescue organizations, and that his shows promoted the importance of the rescue and adoption of homeless dogs. He was interested in meeting Rusty!

Rusty easily passed his audition, and he was adopted by Chris the dog trainer. Now known as Action Jackson, he is performing with other canine agility stars such as Extreme Pepper, Super Sonic, Soaring Sierra, Acrobatic Abby, and Flashy Ferrari in Chris Perondi's Extreme Stunt Dog Show. Their extreme stunts are featured worldwide in live shows, television, film, commercials, and magazines.

Action Jackson's incredible stunts and flying acrobatics now amaze and entertain large audiences. Once homeless and languishing in a shelter, this Jack Russell terrier has become a famous star with extreme talent. Most of all, he is loved and appreciated by his new and perfect owner, Chris.

Hope for Paws was founded in 2008 by Eldad and Audrey Hagar. The couple opened their home in Los Angeles to rescue and have fostered over three hundred dogs, at risk and in distress, from city shelters and off the streets. The animals are provided with emergency aid, medical care, and rehabilitation. Their book, *Our Lives Have Gone to the Dogs*, is a wonderful account and photographer's journey of many of their rescues. All of the money earned from the sales of this book goes directly to helping rescued animals. It may be purchased online at their Web site, http://www.hopeforpaws.org. To watch videos of Action Jackson and other rescue canine stars, go to http://www.extremecanines.com.

Sunshine Mommy Saves a Life with Love, Prayers, and Devotion

In May of 2009, a year-old pug was found by a family on the streets of Anaheim. Unfortunately, they did not realize how sick he really was and did not contact the Pugs 'N Pals rescue organization until three weeks later. He was emaciated at nine pounds, and the rescue was told that he had a severe infection. The Pugs 'N Pals named him Ryan, and they consulted with their veterinarian. Dr. R confirmed that he had a stomach blockage and liver problems, and that he desperately needed surgery. So began the heroic efforts to save his life and the pleas for financial help. Ryan had several surgeries over the course of several months, and he almost died several times. Tina was his foster mom and around-the-clock caregiver. She sang to him "You Are My Sunshine" nearly every day during those difficult times. A portion of Ryan's story is told by excerpts from e-mails sent from Tina to her Pugs 'N Pals volunteers:

> May 26, 2007 2:49 PM
> Well, this little guy is not doing well. We are unsure that we can save him. As you can see by the pic, there is no life left in him. I gave him lots of kisses and told him there is an entire team pulling for him and that he *must* fight.
>
> So pray for little Ryan, as he is touch and go. I will go every day this weekend to visit him and give him encouragement, and to let him know that someone *does* care for his life and that he is loved. Hopefully that will help; it always did in the past. — T.

> May 27, 2007 11:44 AM
> I called today at 9:00 AM, and he was still alive and resting comfortably. I will be going to visit him today to give him encouragement and our lucky blanket. It has been a long, emotional night, and I am beyond exhausted.
>
> Dr. Kim said as we were hanging up, "Thank you guys for doing this for the little one … I don't know of anyone who would go this far." I guess he doesn't know us. —T.

> May 28, 2007 1:13 AM
> He was not responsive to me, but I still gave him lots of kisses, massaged his body to stimulate him, and put the blanket around him to keep him warm. Also, the blanket has my smell, so

hopefully he will start associating it with me when I visit every day.

Please keep him in your thoughts and prayers. He is one of the most critical we've had since Kingsley. —T.

May 29, 2007 11:58 AM

I had to go the Garden Grove to pick up plasma for Dr. R, as he didn't have anyone to go get it, and he needs it right away. Ryan cries all of the time like he's hurting, or maybe is not aware he's doing it. It is really sad to see. I just cry every time I see him, and it breaks my heart to see him in this condition. *What is wrong with people ...* they can get a dog so sick and not do anything about it? —T.

May 29, 2007 3:15 PM

I'll be picking him up around 5:30 and taking him to the ER, and then back to get him at 7:00 AM. Hopefully we can pull him around to be able to deal with all of the other problems that he has. If he makes it, and I pray with all of my heart that he does, he will probably be one of our most incredible miracles.

Please keep him in your prayers, as he is going through a very difficult time right now. —T.

May 29, 2007 7:28 PM

Just left Ryan at the ER, and I left with tears of happiness. He was standing a bit; recognized me and gave me three kisses!!! I just started sobbing. It is better than anything I could get. I'm so happy at the moment; been waiting for this for four days now. He also ate a little bit on his own twice today and didn't throw up!! Yeah!! That's our boy! —T.

May 30, 2007 8:40 AM

Ryan is doing GREAT! I picked him up this morning, and when he saw me the tail started wagging and his eyes lit up and he gave me many kisses. Everyone at the ER started clapping; so many people rooting for this guy. He ate very well last night and is keeping the food down. He still has a long way to go, but he's standing and walking on his own! Yeah!! Here are the pictures that I took this morning. What a difference, hey?!? —T.

May 31, 2007 4:46 PM

I can't believe that this is the same dog that held his lifeless body this weekend. He is skin and bones; the worst I have seen so far, but he is doing so well. He ran around the yard and peed blood, but we're working on it.

He has to eat four to five small meals a day and has *tons* of meds around the clock. No sleep around here!

They bathed him at Dr. R's, and he was filthy. Everyone came out to give him kisses, and he kissed each and every one of them as if to say, "Thank you so much for saving my life."

Thank you everyone for your thoughts and prayers. Keep them coming! —T.

Author's Note: *Ryan has made a 100 percent comeback and now weighs nineteen pounds. When found, his hair was tan; now it is silver. He is expected to live a normal life span of fifteen plus years or more. Ryan is now in a loving home with two other pugs that were also adopted from Pugs 'N Pals. He is loved, happy, and his family* *knows how very special he is. His sunshine mommy misses him; she cried for weeks after he was adopted.*

Pugs 'N Pals has been in operation since 1998 and is a network of nonpaid volunteers dedicated to rescuing pugs, pug mixes, and other small dogs to provide them a second chance at life. They operate throughout Los Angeles, San Diego, Palm Springs, and Kern County and rescue from county shelters, the streets, and owner turn-ins, which have substantially increased in this economy. Pugs are one of the higher maintenance breeds, and this rescue organization is experiencing almost a doubling of their case load from a year ago. Tina Seri, president, would like the public to know that a donation of any amount is very helpful and welcome at this time.

Pugs 'N Pals offers memberships from twenty-five to one hundred dollars per year that can include a newsletter, an invitation to all events, a discount on their merchandise, and special recognition in promotions. The Pug Shop offers items online. Their largest annual fundraiser is PUGTOBERFEST, which features a costumed parade, contests, vendors, food, a raffle and silent auction, and dog services. It is extremely well attended, and some attendees come from out of state. PUGTOBERFEST takes place on the first Saturday of October. For more information, visit their Web site at http://www.pugdogrescue.com.

A Time for Healing

The most endearing things about most American cocker spaniels are their cheerful dispositions, long and velvety-soft feathered ears, and round, dark-colored eyes. When Terri from Tri-Valley Animal Rescue found a stray, young female cocker spaniel in the Tracy Animal Shelter, the dog's demeanor, eyes, and ears told another story—one of pain and suffering. The blonde-colored cocker spaniel suffered ear infections so severe that both ears had abscessed, and it was probable that her hearing was gone. Her medical needs were extraordinary, and she stood no chance of adoption or surviving in the Tracy shelter.

Terri was struck by her sweet disposition despite her terrible affliction, and she appeared to be no more than eighteen months of age. Terri felt compelled to act quickly; the blonde cocker spaniel needed immediate medical attention and surgery—fast. It was February 16, 2009, two days past Valentine's Day, and it proved to be the cocker's lucky day! Terri completed the adoption paperwork and carried her out of the shelter. They were soon in Dr. Tim's office, the veterinarian surgical specialist in Dublin, California, to determine the severity of the infection and come up with a game plan. Dr. Tim advised Terri that her ear infection was the worst that he'd ever seen, and that there was irreversible damage to the ear canals. She needed delicate surgery to remove both diseased ear canals, called total ear canal ablation. The doctor also suspected that one ear might contain cancer. She stood a chance of a total recovery but would be totally deaf for the rest of her life.

The powers that be at Tri-Valley Rescue were undaunted. This beautiful, sweet dog they named Kylie would make someone a wonderful pet. Antibiotics were started immediately and the surgery proved to be successful. Cancer was found in one ear, but the surgeon and pathologist later called to say that they felt that they had removed all of it. Their Cinderella Funds, created for dogs in extraordinary need through annual fundraisers, picked up the surgery bill for two thousand dollars.

It was decided that Kylie should now enjoy a new quality of life, and she was not subjected to radiation or chemotherapy treatments. She eventually went home to heal with Terri, her new foster mom. Terri knew that it would take an extraordinary family to adopt a dog that was not only deaf but had the possibility of a future bout with cancer. As many months passed, she vowed that if they could not find Kylie a new family, she would keep her.

And then in the fall of 2009, the perfect person appeared: another cancer survivor who had endured not one but thirty reconstructive surgical procedures after a bout with cancer to his face. He was Terry Healey, a local businessman and professional speaker, author, and board member of the Cancer League, Inc. His popular lecture series includes such topics as navigating life's road blocks, turning points and survivor kits, dealing with adversity and taking control of your life, and embracing our differences. He's the author of *At Face Value: My Triumph over a Disfiguring Cancer* by Caveat Press, and a contributing author to three other books. Terry has appeared in dozens of national and local TV networks and has been interviewed on more than seventy-five radio stations across the United States and Canada.

Terry and his wife, Sue, were looking for a companion to their yellow Labrador retriever named Janelle. Terry had previously seen a rescue dog advertisement with a picture of Kylie's face. When he read the story about this little cancer survivor, he was struck with feelings of sympathy and familiarity. He showed the ad to his wife.

Terry exclaimed, "Kylie looks just like me. The right side of her face is disfigured from cancer, and her right eye droops, just like mine!"

Sue pondered on these things, and the following day she approached Terry and remarked, "You were given a second chance, and I think Kylie deserves a second chance."

After visiting with Kylie and her foster mom, Sue asked Terry to join her on a second visit. They adopted Kylie that very day. A favorite female name of Terry's is Kaleigh, and that became her name.

Kaleigh became comfortable in her new surroundings and enjoyed the company of her new big sister, Janelle. Janelle, a yellow Labrador retriever, was a career change dog from Guide Dogs for the Blind. Janelle was very gentle with Kaleigh and accepted her immediately. Now totally deaf, the cocker spaniel crawled and leaned next to Janelle, not just to rest, but to feel Janelle's movement. It was her way of being alerted when someone entered the room or when the doorbell rang. Her new and joyful life included weekend visits to Tahoe Donner in Truckee, California. Terry and Sue have a cabin, and their time together consisted of walks in the pine forests, swims at Donner Lake, and rides across the lake on a paddleboard.

But in October of 2009, they discovered another lump. Her cancer returned, and the couple sought advice from the UC Davis Veterinary Center. Kaleigh then underwent sixteen treatments of radiation, and at the time of writing this is in the midst of six months of chemotherapy. Sue reports that the dog's energy is amazing and that she is still "full of spit and vinegar."

Terry and Sue believe that there are magical forces in the universe that have been at work and continue for Kaleigh's benefit. Consider this: A volunteer by the name of TERRI from Tri-Valley Animal Rescue was Kaleigh's foster mom. A cancer survivor by the name of TERRY is now her permanent dad. The director of this rescue organization responsible for her rescue from the shelter is named Lisa HEALy. Terry's last name is HEALey. Terry's nickname in college, before he contracted cancer, was HEALS. The Healeys, and certainly this author, are of the opinion that Kaleigh has found her way to exactly the right people who can love her and help her in her HEALing.

Tri-Valley Animal Rescue (TVAR) was founded in 1992 and is a nonprofit charitable organization located in Dublin, California, whose mission is to end the unnecessary euthanasia of homeless animals. TVAR is 100 percent volunteer, 250 members strong, and cooperates with East County Animal Shelter in Dublin, other surrounding shelters, and local rescue groups. They ensure that at-risk, treatable, and adoptable animals are rescued from these specific shelters. Their efforts provide for routine and special needs medical care, foster care, and socialization of the animals. TVAR matches suitable, responsible new owners with animals through adoption events. Their programs provide low-cost spay/neuter programs and educate the public about responsible pet ownership. TVAR rescues over one thousand animals every year.

Their Cinderella Fund is used to specifically save dogs with extraordinary needs and transform them into wonderful pets.

Special events include Maddie's Matchmaker Adopt-a-thons and Claws for Paws. Online shopping features customized pet portraits, custom shirts, and fine paw print jewelry. For more information, visit their Web site at http://www.tvar.org.

Rescued from a Walmart Parking Lot

Author's Note: *This is the story about a rescue volunteer for NorCal Irish Setter Rescue, who made a split-second decision to come to the aid of four golden retriever puppies during the Christmas season. She understood that puppies are fragile and may have compromised immune systems, particularly if they've not been vaccinated. A parking lot was not a healthy place for them to be.*

In December of 2008, a dog owner and canine rescue volunteer by the name of Ki (pronounced K-eye) was running errands in Tracy. She had her dog, Emma, in the car, as plans included taking Emma to the groomer and later to the obedience trainer. But Ki had a few minutes to spare and decided to stop by Walmart to buy Christmas cards. It was three in the afternoon and a cool, brisk day in Northern California. She spied three people on a park bench near the door, as well as what appeared to be four puppies: two on the bench and two on the ground, no blankets, no water bowls, no collars, no leashes. She decided to duck inside Walmart and call her friend, Gina, to share the news of the puppies in peril.

"Can you believe this?? I've got to do something."

She turned and quickly walked back outside. By this time, a small group of interested onlookers had gathered to inspect and play with the puppies, who appeared to be purebred golden retrievers. She boldly pushed her way to the front to speak to the young couple and an older woman, who appeared to be a mother of one of the two.

"Are you selling these puppies?" Ki asked.

"Yes."

"Really? Have they had their shots?"

"No."

"Why not?"

"We can't afford it."

"Do you own the parents? Are they golden retrievers?"

"Yes."

"What are you selling them for?"

"$150 each."

By this time, a family came over to inquire about the puppies, and Ki realized that time was of the essence. She took a step forward and postured herself in front of them and other onlookers.

"I want all four. I believe that's six hundred dollars."

Now, she had to come up with six hundred dollars, and quickly. There was a Bank of America nearby, and maybe they would cash a check for her. But would the sellers wait? A few more onlookers stopped to admire the puppies.

She turned to them. "I have friends with NORCAL Golden Retriever Rescue, and I know that they will find the dogs good homes. Don't buy these puppies! They haven't had their shots."

She left quickly and drove to the Bank of America, praying that the puppies would still be there when she got back. She also called her husband, Mark, and he agreed to the transaction. The bank accepted her check; she cashed it, and returned to find the puppies were still there. The couple was thrilled to receive the cash, and Ki intuitively suspected that something wasn't right. *Why are there only four puppies? Litters are always bigger; these must be the leftovers,* she thought.

Ki had no crate or way of transporting them safely. Her own dog, Emma, was in her own crate in the back seat, and she couldn't expose the puppies to the older dog. She persuaded the couple, with mother in tow, to follow her in their truck with the puppies to Gina's house. There she put Emma in the fenced-in backyard for safekeeping and carefully tucked the puppies into Emma's crate. She gave them water, which they drank voraciously.

The previous owners left in their truck, and Ki hit the freeway. Her veterinarian, Dr. James, was forty-five minutes away in San Ramon. During the drive, she called volunteers she knew from NORCAL Golden Retriever Rescue to let them know that she had obtained four puppies that needed immediate foster care and was on the way to the vet for shots and exams. She needed h-e-l-p! As she drove, the puppies slept, exhausted from their day in the parking lot.

Four veterinarian technicians rushed to greet them as she walked in with the crate of precious cargo. They set to work to identify each puppy with a red, blue, yellow, or green collar, and Dr. James determined that they were eight to ten weeks old. They received the critical de-worming and parvo immunizations, and each was given a Nylabone and a toy. Ki was given six cans of special puppy food, as they were surely hungry.

She packed them up again and loaded them into her station wagon. Now it was home to Walnut Creek, and her husband, Mark, was waiting to help. They would care for the puppies overnight, and the golden retriever rescue volunteers would take them in the morning.

Ki and Mark blocked off an eight-foot-by-eight-foot area in the kitchen, and put down newspapers and towels. A gated outside patio served as the puppies' pee and poop area, which was used quite frequently!

During the next few hours the puppies were fed and bathed. Ki bathed them one at a time in the kitchen sink, and Mark carefully rubbed them with towels, until they were dry and fluffy. By 10:30, everyone was exhausted. The puppies were put to bed in the kitchen and, miraculously, they all slept quietly from 11:00 PM–6:00 AM.

Later that morning, they were surrendered to three volunteers of NORCAL Golden Retriever Rescue. Ki and Mark would not accept a reimbursement of six hundred dollars from NORCAL, but instead asked that the money be considered a donation. The puppies all found wonderful homes and were named Moses, Riley, Rowan, and Darwin.

Ki commented: "Rescuing those four golden retriever puppies was the best Christmas gift we could have ever had. We literally glowed for weeks! Every year we set aside money for a charity, which we give at Christmas time. That year we had less to give than usual, and we hadn't decided on what organization to bestow it. It was absolutely meant to be!"

And the amount of money that they saved to give away? You guessed it: six hundred dollars!

NORCAL Golden Retriever Rescue is an all-volunteer organization founded in 1989, originating from the NORCAL Golden Retriever Club. Their mission is to rescue and place adoptable golden retrievers in Northern California in safe, loving homes, thereby improving the lives of both the dog and the adoption household. NORCAL has over one hundred volunteers throughout Northern California, and they rescue approximately four hundred dogs a year, operating from Fresno to the Oregon border and the Lake Tahoe/Reno area.

Placement services are offered for owners who need to give up their dogs because of changing life circumstances, such as relocation, financial hardship, divorce, allergies, illness, or death. They also rescue abandoned, neglected, and abused goldens, as well as seniors (those over eight years old). NORCAL accepts bonded pairs, even if only one is a purebred golden retriever. They also provide long-term care for dogs with special needs who are hard to place, and compassionate, pain-free hospice care for dogs where medical treatment is no longer appropriate. Surgery is provided for orthopedic and other problems with a good prognosis for recovery. Expenses are primarily veterinary care, neutering and spaying, transportation, and administration.

An annual fundraising event includes an art and wine auction. Also, an online store features, among other things: calendars, totes, backpacks, caps, shirts, jackets, and towels with golden retriever logos. A quarterly newsletter is available online. For more information, visit http://www.ngrr.org.

Georgia Peach Attends Special Olympics

Georgia was surrendered by her owners to the Southern California Newfoundland Rescue (SCNR) in January 2008, and she has been their "Georgia Peach" ever since. She's a massive hunk of love weighing more than one hundred pounds and is kind, gentle, and happy virtually all of the time. A Newfoundland's sweet temperament is known as the hallmark of the breed. Georgia has a unique appearance: predominantly black with a white chest and white paws with black polka dots.

Newfoundlands were first bred from Newfoundland Island by British and French fisherman. These gentle giants have a love of water and are strong swimmers. In Europe, they are used as lifeguards to save swimmers in distress.

Georgia, however, cannot swim due to a common disorder called laryngeal paralysis that causes difficulty with breathing and swallowing. It typically occurs in larger breed dogs. Luckily, she had surgery on her throat and is better now, and she wades in a swimming pool to cool off on hot days. She also had surgeries on both of her knees and has a heart condition that her veterinarian monitors.

Georgia can't be an athlete, but she's able to support them by just being her lovable, social self. Every year she attends the Special Olympics Summer Games at Cal State Long Beach. Events include swimming, track and field, basketball, gymnastics, and tennis. The Newfoundland Club of Southern California has participated for more than twenty years. They have a booth at the Olympic village, where the athletes can interact with the dogs, sit with them, and get their pictures taken with them. Georgia poses well for the pictures and gives them kisses. In fact, she's so photogenic and people-oriented that she is the poster dog of the Southern California Newfoundland Rescue, attending all fundraisers and rescue functions when required.

When Georgia is not representing her rescue organization at special events, her other important job is that of Nana in *Peter Pan*, a children's playmate and protector to her two-year-old boy, named Tyler, and baby, Rebecca. They live a few blocks away in Costa Mesa from her beloved foster mom, Laurie, who gave up Georgia for adoption in April 2008.

When Georgia returns home from her "gigs" with Laurie, Tyler is waiting for her at the front door and shouts, "My doggy is home!" He proclaims this while clutching his black, stuffed Newfie dog that resembles his gentle giant.

"Miss Georgia or G is so good with our kids it's ridiculous," Tyler's mom, Megan, says. "She has a lot of energy and a lot of personality. She purposely lies in the doorways so that as you go by you have to pat her on the head, and Tyler has to crawl over her to get from room to room. Any giggling and she's running in there to play, too. In the mornings, we get Tyler out of bed by saying, 'Time to give Georgia a hug!' Works like a charm."

Southern California Newfoundland Rescue (SCNR) is a service provided by the Newfoundland Club of Southern California, a regional club of the Newfoundland Club of America. All members of rescue are volunteers. Newfoundlands are acquired from animal shelters or surrendered by owners who can no longer keep them. This rescue tries to be the adopting party on all animal shelter dogs, so that it can assess health and temperament, properly groom, and facilitate adoption into an appropriate home. Surrendered dogs may be returned to breeders. If the breeder cannot be found or the dog is refused by the breeder, it will be fostered. SCNR spays or neuters all fostered dogs. The dogs also receive all necessary medical attention and are micro-chipped so that they are permanently identified and linked to the organization. SCNR is supported by adoption donations, merchandise sales, club functions, and personal donations from Newfie lovers. For more information, visit their Web site at http://www.newfclubofsocal.com/rescue.

Setting Up Max for Success

Author's Note: *Marti is the founder of Bichon FurKids Rescue (BFK) in La Costa, California. She has been a bichon frise owner since 1977. Ten years later, she adopted her second bichon after responding to a newspaper ad for a four-year-old female. It was love at first sight! Samantha happily walked down the sidewalk with her new owner and never looked back. Then in the car, she laid in Marti's lap and thanked her. The following year included a successful cataract surgery. They had fourteen wonderful years together. In 2001, brokenhearted after the death of Samantha, Marti got involved with rescue by fostering a tear-stained and matted bichon that she named Lindsey. The condition of poor Lindsey and the needs of so many other bichons to be rescued and fostered into loving homes compelled Marti to start her own organization.*

Marti's family consists of rescued bichons Lindsey, Missy, Max, and any temporary Fur Kid passing through. It is the caregiver and mediator Lindsey that makes the other dogs in Marti's home welcome and comfortable, particularly Max. This is Max's story.

It was a chilly November morning in 2007, just before Thanksgiving. A tiny, traumatized, and malnourished bichon puppy was found in a veterinarian's drop box in Kearny Mesa. Sadly, he had spent the night in a cold, dark, wooden box meant for medications and donations. The lab technicians named him Max, and the three-month-old puppy became their personal project. He received tender loving care and food, water, a bath, and preliminary shots.

In less than a week and weighing less than eight pounds, Max was neutered and declared healthy. He was then given to another veterinarian in La Jolla, as it was hoped that someone within his practice might be interested in adopting him. Luckily, a bichon owner spied Max and called Marti and asked her to take him and find him a home. Marti picked him up two days later, intending to foster Max until a forever home could be found.

The cute and cuddly puppy appeared to be the typical bichon frise with white, fluffy fur, big brown eyes, and a round, black nose. This breed was popular during the Middle Ages in France, Italy, and England and accepted into the American Kennel Club approximately sixty years ago. Bichons are loving, playful, obedient, and great with children and other pets.

Max was properly groomed and prepared for adoption, and a wonderful home was found. But it was not to last. Marti and Max's trainer noticed that he exhibited "fly catching" behavior, which is typical for dogs with epilepsy and nervous system disorders.

After consultation with Dr. Jeff and others, Max was diagnosed with hepatic microvascular dysplasia, or MVD. MVD is a liver disease found in many small breeds. Dogs with the disease may be normal in appearance most of the time, but can have intermittent problems. Dr. Jeff further explained to Marti that he would be bothered by loud noises and moving things: cars, skateboards, vacuum cleaners, and people moving quickly around him or coming toward him. Max was put on a special diet to help his liver perform as well as possible and given homeopathic medications to support the liver and nervous system.

The puppy that had been discarded in a drop box was now in need of special care for the rest of his life. Marti realized that she could help Max with the problems associated with MVD, and that Max would thrive in a forever home with Lindsay and Missy. Max would become Marti's teacher, and with her help, he steadily improved.

Since learning about the disease and how to cope with it, there have been two other rescued bichons and a poodle who have come across Marti's path with the same disease. Now, as a result of her experience and knowledge of medications, she is able to help other dogs and their owners cope with MVD and sound and motion sensitivities.

At times when his nervous system gets overloaded, Marti has to be on guard and watchful. Marti explained, "When I anticipate visitors or new experiences in my home, I have Max wear a citronella collar called Spray Commander. It's designed to stop inappropriate behavior or nuisance barking; it beeps and delivers a small or large spritz of fragrance under Max's chin. He doesn't care for the beep or the spray, so now I simply put the collar on and he acts more subdued. He's watchful and careful not to receive a single beep!"

Marti also uses dog appeasing pheromone (DAP) diffusers throughout her house, which serve to mellow dogs that have stress of any kind. Max even tolerates the gardener with his noisy machines.

Thankfully, with proper treatment of the disease, Max is full grown at fourteen pounds and is happy, playful, and medically stable. Marti reports that every day he and Lindsey do the "Bichon Buzz"—mad dashes in figure eights throughout the house and barking, as if to say, "I'm so-o happy! Here I come!"

Bichon FurKids Rescue (BFK) was founded in 2006 and is comprised of 150 volunteers located in Southern California, Northern California, Nevada, and Arizona. They are dedicated to rescuing bichons, bichon mixes, and other small dogs with physical, medical, and emotional needs that can no longer live with their original guardians and need forever homes. They rescued more than eight hundred dogs from 2007 to 2008 and re-homed over four hundred in 2009. BFK volunteers believe that each life is meaningful, and that all "Fur Kids" deserve to live out their lives as loving companions. Their motto, "Making a difference in a dog's life," reflects this desire in their willingness to foster, transport, and assist in the effort to rescue and re-home. As part of their mission, they educate the community regarding the necessity to eradicate puppy mills, the importance of spaying and neutering pets, and how to be responsible pet guardians.

Fundraising activities include a new e-Bay store and their online Web site boutique of clothing and home and office accessories that carry the FurKids Rescue logo. BFK also has a relationship with Amazon.com, Ralphs, and Washington Mutual. For every item purchased, BFK receives a small percentage of sales. All proceeds are applied to the vetting and caring for rescued bichons and other small dogs in need. Their bimonthly newsletter, *Bichon Bits and Bytes,* is available online. For more information, visit http://www.bichonfurkids.org.

A Home for Zoey

Author's Note: *Dogs are routinely scorned and euthanized in some county shelters because they are not totally dog social around certain breeds and sizes of other dogs. Uninformed humans think that dogs who do not always get along with other dogs will be discriminating about people, and it's just not the case. Zoey has never met a person, big or small, that she didn't adore!*

Zoey sat at the kennel door in the Monterey County Animal Shelter every day and smiled at everyone passing by. But no one took an interest in her; she was a very photogenic and good-natured Heinz 57 of many things, possibly husky, pit bull, akita,

Dalmatian, and border collie. Black and white, she resembled Petey the dog, made popular in the fifties television show *Our Gang* with the Little Rascals. But after two months, her time at the shelter ran out and she was put on the euthanasia list. A volunteer from Animal Friends Rescue Project (AFRP) who monitored dogs with no time left stepped up and saved her.

Animal Friends was inundated with dogs and could not find Zoey a foster home because, despite her loving, sweet disposition with humans, she didn't do well around small dogs. She was placed in a spacious kennel, and AFRP rescue volunteers played with her and exercised her nearly every day. The kennel had an exercise yard for supervised play groups with other large dogs, which she very much enjoyed. It was unclear whether she was house trained, and she needed to be walked on a leash by an adult because she was large and lacked obedience training. She was less than one year old.

Weeks turned into months and despite her cuteness, few people were interested. Two families inquired about her, but she was not exactly what they wanted and needed in a dog. The Animal Friends volunteers now hoped and prayed for a perfect home for her.

Fortunately, the third time was the charm, and her luck changed. The Matabuena family of five saw Zoey's smiling face on the Animal Friends Web site. They were in love and really didn't care what her specific breed heritage was. They had been looking for a family dog for some time and just had not made the right connection. The Matabuenas immediately filled out an application.

There were several telephone calls and e-mails between the family and AFRP to make sure that they understood the adoption process and to discuss all of Zoey's personality traits, history, training, and general care needs. A volunteer from Pug Rescue of Sacramento (PROS) who lived in their area agreed to perform the home check, which they passed. The family made plans to drive from their home in the East Bay.

It was December 1, 2007, a rainy day and Mrs. Matabuena's birthday. They all piled into their minivan and drove two hours to the AFRP Adoption Center in Pacific Grove to meet Zoey and her rescue coordinator, Gina. The Matabuena children, Kyle, Alexis, and Joshua, ages seven, four, and three, respectively, played with her, and then they all took her for a long walk. The whole family was smitten by Zoey, and after a year she was finally going home with a new, loving family as a companion and watchdog for three children.

Gina and other Animal Friends volunteers were pleased that a loving, sweet dog found a perfect home with lots of attention from the children, and the Matabuenas report that she returns every bit of it. Edwin said, "She loves to dig in the backyard and bury things, and leaves mud circles with her nose on the sliding back door. Zoey's been a jogging companion with me on weekends and follows the kids around as a playmate and protector … and she's a big-time kisser! Zoey is such a great dog for us. We feel that it was destiny that she came into our lives when she did."

Animal Friends Rescue Project (AFRP) was founded in 1998 by four individuals who were passionate about making a difference to companion animal overpopulation. AFRP is based in Pacific Grove and is dedicated to finding permanent homes for abandoned, stray, and abused companion animals, and ending the pet overpopulation crisis through a focused spay/neuter voucher program called Prevent-a-Litter (PAL). They primarily rescue animals at risk of euthanasia from the City of Salinas Animal Shelter and the Monterey County Animal Shelter. Other rescue priorities are given to Santa Cruz and San Benito counties. They have also been called to help in other areas, including Los Banos, San Jose, Stockton, Tulare, Merced, and Bakersfield. AFRP has the reputation in the community for taking the "least adoptable" animals from shelters, giving them the time and medical attention they need, and finding them good, permanent homes. Adoptable animals are shown on the Web site and newsletter. AFRP is led by an active board of directors and a dedicated staff. They rely on approximately three hundred volunteers.

Annual fundraising events include the Holiday Party Fundraiser and Party for the Paws, also benefitting Friends of County Services (FOCAS) and Salinas Animal Services. AFRP also operates a Treasure Shop in Pacific Grove, and AFRP merchandise and Art for Animals are available online. Their newsletter, *Animal Friends Update*, is available online and through e-mail. For more information, visit http://www.animalfriendsrescue.org.

Trouble Continues His Mission to Help a Son with Special Needs

Author's Note: *Kathy is the Southern California volunteer representative for the U.S. national organization Russell Rescue, Inc. She's in charge of a dozen fostered dogs at any given time, coordinates the shelter rescues and subsequent transport, and fields calls for help in finding Jack Russell terriers. She works with four other volunteers to handle these responsibilities. Kathy was at this job for only a few months when the following scenario took place. She now understands that rescuers are guided and used by the powers that be to facilitate the "perfect match," and a Craigslist advertisement was the key to making that happen.*

A family from Ceres in Northern California contacted Kathy about the need to replace a deceased and beloved Jack Russell for companionship with their fifteen-year-old autistic son. (This was a very unusual request, for a Jack Russell's personality is usually not appropriate for a special needs child.) The son wanted an exact duplication of what he had with his past beloved Russell: black and white with a broken coat (smooth to rough), and the dog had to like water (most don't). It was a very tall order!

By happenstance (or was it?), Kathy read a Craigslist advertisement several months later concerning the immediate need to find a home for a Jack Russell terrier whose owner was moving to Japan. The ad described the dog owner as a learning and behavioral specialist for autistic children. Her four-year-old dog named Trouble slept with her autistic son and happily coexisted with as many as twenty autistic children in her house at any given time. She was soon leaving for Japan to continue her work with special needs children and their families coping with the disorder, and could not bring her special Jack Russell terrier with her. She desperately needed to find her dog a new owner, and fast!

Kathy wasn't feeling well with the flu but remembered the family that had contacted her, wanting a black-and-white, broken-coated Russell that tolerated autistic children. But that was asking for the moon! What were the chances that this dog was black and white, smooth to rough, and liked water? She contacted the owner of Trouble anyway and, sure enough, found out that he was indeed black and white, had a broken coat, and "was in our pool all of the time." Bingo! Perfect match!

Kathy hurriedly contacted the family in Northern California to tell them that she had somehow found them the Russell that matched their exact description and provided them with the Craigslist information. Then she contacted the woman who placed the advertisement, told her about the family in Nor Cal, and provided her with their phone number.

Kathy was so ill that she was not well enough to prepare the adoption paperwork, should things progress to that point. She related, "Days went by and I didn't hear from either one of them. Neither party returned my phone calls. I thought that somehow things hadn't worked out, and that the opportunity to make it happen was lost. I knew that the owner of Trouble had already moved to Japan. I was devastated."

Then one day out of the blue, there appeared a $200 online donation to Russell Rescue, Inc. from Trouble's new family. It was the exact amount of an adoption fee. She later learned that both families connected with her help, and knowing that she was ill with the flu, they went ahead and finalized their plans for Trouble. Things were going perfectly!

The adoption paperwork was signed, sealed, and delivered. Trouble was now officially the new buddy and companion of their fifteen-year-old son with special needs.

"She's even better than anyone could ever imagine! You found us the perfect dog!" Trouble's new mom exclaimed in an e-mail, and she thanked Kathy for facilitating the "chance introduction" of Trouble from an advertisement on Craigslist.

"I guess it's all in a day's work," Kathy quoted to this author. "Trouble's mission in life is to continue doing what he was initially trained for and is best at doing. How wonderful it is to be involved in facilitating his mission in special needs … with a new family!"

Russell Rescue, Inc. (RRI) is a national network of volunteers dedicated to placing Jack Russell terriers that are no longer wanted or have been placed in county shelters. RRI provides medical care before adoption and finds suitable homes for all terriers in their care. All dogs entering rescue are temporarily placed in foster homes, or they must remain with their owners until suitable homes are found. Foster space is limited, and foster homes are generally reserved for dogs that are in danger of euthanasia at local shelters or are in emergency situations. RRI has established a relationship with PetPlan USA, a Philadelphia-based pet health company. RRI strongly believes in the health and welfare of all pets throughout their lives. Good and affordable pet insurance is an important component of responsible, caring ownership.

RRI is funded entirely by donations. These donations are used for temporary housing, spaying/neutering, shipping to new homes, veterinarian care, food, and water. Fundraising activities include eBay Giving Works Donation Program, a Russell Rescue Internet store, and eBay auctions with Russell apparel and gift items. For more information, visit their Web site at http://www.russellrescue.com.

Loving Humans and Canines Conquer Adversity in Guam

Author's Note: *Volunteers Noni and Dave from Guam Animals in Need worked with a number of greyhound rescue organizations from the United States, including Homestretch Rescue and Adoption in Fillmore, California. Our thanks also go to the Greyhound Protection League, who funded the Guam veterinary care and the airfare for the dogs.*

Noni didn't realize that her life with canine rescue started on the day that Dave proposed marriage—with blueberry muffins and a new, red Miata sports car. All for her! She was so impressed with his creativity and love for her that she accepted. She promptly moved from her home in China to Dave's in Guam, and they were married in November 2000. Two world travelers, sixty-three and seventy-three years of age, who met on a dating Web site, proved to be a match made in heaven.

She was originally from South Africa, and he was a retired engineer from the U.S. Air Force. Dave immediately introduced her to a friend who was involved with Guam Animals in Need (GAIN). With no experience with animals or animal rescue, Noni became involved as well, and together the married couple shared their passion for helping Guam's at-risk "jungle dogs."

Everything changed on November 28, 2008. A dog racetrack closed, and the owner suddenly announced over the radio that greyhounds would be given away to the general public. Hundreds of people showed up for free animals, thinking that they would be useful as guard dogs. It was total chaos: no screening, no adoption paperwork, no new owner names and phone numbers. Several hundred greyhounds were reportedly turned out that day.

GAIN and Noni sprang into action, despite the fact that they had no knowledge or experience with the greyhound breed. Noni took ten dogs, three at a time, and kennels were found for them. They had bald spots and skin infections from lying on concrete in their kennels, but otherwise they appeared to be healthy.

In December, GAIN volunteers began finding many depressed and starving greyhounds on the street, and they were getting reports from citizens regarding "sightings." The animals were abandoned because they did not make good guard dogs. Greyhounds are nonbarkers, lazy, gentle, and sweet souls, best described as "forty-five miles per hour couch potatoes." Noni and Dave were distraught.

One day a sighting of three greyhounds was reported by a worker at a coral quarry on the eastern side of the island. Dave and Noni knew it to be a remote tourist attraction "cave area" surrounded by dense jungle vegetation. The worker directed them to an intersection where he kindly waited for them. Together they walked into the quarry and found two very weak, dehydrated, and emaciated dogs: a white-and-tan girl and a charcoal gray boy. Thankfully they were still alive; the boy barely so.

Dave and Noni carried the two dogs to their van and gave them food and water, but the dogs were too weak to eat and only drank a small amount. The girl helplessly looked on as the boy stared into her eyes. A heart-bonded couple had managed to survive the jungle together. It was right then and there that Dave and Noni decided to name the boy Marbo, after nearby Marbo Cave, and the girl Mabel.

Dave and Noni rushed the greyhounds to the nearest veterinarian. They were given IVs, medication, and small, frequent meals. After five days, they were taken back to the GAIN shelter, still weak and frail.

Three days later, Marbo was reported to be in trouble, and Noni rushed to the shelter. A retired nurse, she inserted an IV and loaded him into her van. En route to the veterinarian, she noticed he wasn't breathing. She pulled off the road and, not feeling a pulse, performed CPR. After a few minutes, Marbo gasped and began breathing again. She got back into the driver's seat and drove, all the time glancing back to where Marbo was lying.

He stopped breathing a few more times, but he responded again to CPR and prayers. Noni knew that she needed help, and by cell phone called two GAIN volunteers, Amber and Rosa, who intercepted them on the road. They climbed into the car and rolled Marbo for stimulation to keep his heart beating. He would make it now.

Marbo was admitted to the vet's office and given more IV fluids, medications, and a special diet, but he was terribly depressed and not eating. Noni realized that he was missing his girlfriend Mabel, so she brought the dog over to visit Marbo. Like magic, the visit cheered him up and he started eating and drinking!

Three days passed and Marbo was discharged to return to the GAIN shelter to be reunited with Mabel. Marbo perked up. He was given a special diet of yogurt, cooked chicken, vegetables, rice, and evaporated milk. He now needed one-on-one care in a foster home, and Noni realized that these two best friends needed to be together.

Shirley, a volunteer, took Marbo and Mabel into her home and gave them both the TLC that they so desperately needed to recover. The heart-bonded couple spent three months in her warm and loving home. Marbo very slowly came back to life with the proper meds and nourishment.

Noni left Guam for their home in Arizona in February 2009, leaving Dave behind to care for the last of the greyhounds. To date, four dogs are still in rehabilitation and in need of constant care. Dave's job is to finish their care and get them off the island—by air. Noni estimates that they have flown approximately 180 dogs to the United States for new homes! They are now located in the Bay Area, Los Angeles, Seattle, Portland, Alaska, the East Coast, and many states in between, as well as Canada, Hawaii, and Japan.

During the day, Noni and Dave are busy with e-mails to new owners and foster families wanting to know details about their greyhounds. Every night they catch up with each other by cell phone. The loving couple will soon be permanently reunited in Arizona, and Guam will be a distant memory.

Marbo and Mable, the other loving couple, flew back to the States in March 2009. Both dogs were adopted into different forever homes and are now forty-five miles per hour couch potatoes. All is well.

The Homestretch Greyhound Rescue and Adoption finds permanent and loving homes for retired racing greyhounds. While in their care, these beautiful, loyal, and affectionate dogs receive the best in-home training, food, and medical attention. It is their mission to be advocates for greyhounds by providing an environment that contrasts with the difficult conditions the dogs encounter during their racing careers and publicly promoting an end to greyhound racing. Nearly every one of the thirty thousand greyhounds bred each year by the racing industry that survive puppy life will eventually need to be rescued to find a true home. It is estimated that 50 percent of greyhound puppies are euthanized.

Homestretch was heavily involved with the rescue of the 180 dogs from Guam, a U.S. territory, by providing entry services, temporary housing, and medical care. Donations from literally all over the world were used to get the greyhounds off the island, with special thanks to Dave and Noni Davis from Guam. Based in Fillmore, California, Homestretch is run by Barbara Davenport and Bob Smith with the help of many volunteers. To date they have placed over 250 greyhounds in forever homes and received the Canine Adoption and Rescue League's Wags for Wellness Award in 2009.

Homestretch is completely funded by donations that come from the publication of its newsletter, *GreytTimes*. For more information, please go to http://www.homestretchgreys.org and http://www.guamgreyhounds.org.

An Internet Partnership Helps a Dog in Peril Overseas

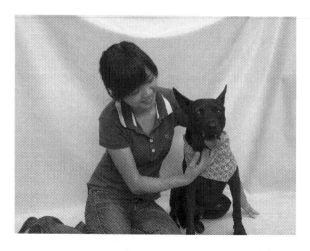

Sadly, there are many puppies abandoned on the streets of Taiwan, and a small black dog of a pure Formosa breed was one of them. He was found lying in the street, dying from a small collar he had outgrown that was virtually choking him. Thanks to an organization in Taiwan called Animal Rescue Team (ART) TAIWAN and Maggie Chen, this lucky dog was rescued and taken to a veterinarian who quickly performed a complicated operation needed to cut away the collar from the skin and relieve his breathing.

On June 3 of 2009, a now healthy Formosa "boy" named Purple arrived at LAX and was happily greeted by Susan from Labs and Buddies Animal Rescue.

Susan commented, "Purple endured a thirty-day quarantine and around-the-world air travel in a mesh crate ... two hours at the Taiwan airport, a seventeen-hour flight, and over an hour in customs. By any stretch of the imagination, any human would have been grouchy and dead tired. When I opened his crate, I was absolutely amazed to find a calm and happy dog with a wagging tail! We are constantly amazed at the resiliency and composure of these dogs after their flights. They seem to know that they're starting a new life and that all is well!"

Now eighteen months old and weighing thirty-five pounds, the jet black dog with tall, upright ears and brown eyes is happy, healed, and leading a new life in Southern California. He's in a loving, safe environment with his foster mom, Laura, from Labs and Buddies. Evidence of his ordeal can only be seen in a cute double chin, excess skin that accumulated around his neck from the small collar.

Formosa dogs are distinctly a Taiwanese breed. They are all black with shiny coats of Labrador-like fur. Formosas have easygoing, sweet, retriever-type personalities, are nonbarkers, loyal, and sociable with humans and other dogs. Dogs like Purple are currently up for adoption and are great with kids and other dogs of any size.

Oh, in case you're wondering why a black dog is named Purple, Formosas have purple tongues! And if Purple could talk, he would thank Maggie, ART's veterinarian, Susan, and Laura for saving his life and giving him a loving home in California.

Editor's Note: *ART TAIWAN has been rescuing and rehabilitating stray animals from the streets since 1995. After a dog has been rehabilitated, they then contact partnering canine rescue organizations in the United States through the Internet, relaying the specific story of a dog and its life-saving surgery and progress* *from pictures. Knowing that these rescued dogs stand virtually no chance of survival in Taiwan, this organization routinely flies dogs into Seattle, San Francisco, and Los Angeles to affiliated rescue organizations along the West Coast. Also, thanks go to the American rescue organizations, for it is their fundraising efforts that pay the six hundred dollars in airfare for each dog.*

Labs and Buddies Animal Rescue (LBAR) is a no-kill rescue in Los Angeles, California, committed to saving all types of Labrador retrievers, Lab mixes, and other mixed breed dogs. They specialize in saving, but not limited to, black dogs from high-kill shelters, and adopting them to loving and qualified homes. (Statistically speaking, black dogs are harder to place, as light-colored dogs are most often preferred.) Currently, this organization is rescuing and finding forever homes for approximately one hundred dogs a year. For more information, visit their Web site at http://www.labsandbuddies.org.

Memories of Emma

Author's Note: *Rescued dogs become grateful, trusting, and loyal family members. This story is about an unhappy dog who found a perfect home. Her new life of happiness spanned the engagement and ten-year marriage of a couple who share a deep passion and commitment to canine rescue.*

She appeared to be a golden retriever mixed with border collie or shepherd, with lots of thick fur the color of cinnamon and a most endearing feature: flying nun ears. But her ears were down, her tail was tucked under her body, and her head was cautiously low to the ground. Her name was, oddly enough, Miss Pearl, and she was six years old. She was available for adoption along with five other dogs by the golden retriever rescue organization, Homeward Bound Golden Retriever and Sanctuary.

It was the annual canine adoption Picnic Day at the UC Davis campus and veterinarian school. Many dogs needing new homes were available, brought by volunteers of California rescue organizations. In April 1999, Sandra and her boyfriend, Bob, were looking for a companion to her dog, Kessie, a twelve-year-old yellow Labrador. When Sandra approached, Miss Pearl uttered a low, steady g-r-r-r-r-r as if to say, "Stay back. I don't trust you!"

From their experience working with rescued animals, the couple understood that she suffered from some sort of abuse and trauma. Unruffled, they introduced her to Kessie by taking both dogs for a long walk. A bonding took place, and they decided that Miss Pearl would come around in time with an understanding and acceptance of her new situation. Sandra and Bob would provide the loving, stable home that she deserved, and Kessie would be a mellow, happy playmate. Adoption paperwork began and they loaded the dogs into their Volvo station wagon and went home to the Bay Area.

With a new life came a new identity. She became Emma, and at times, Miss Emma. Cautious and submissive at first, Emma slowly relaxed and gained trust in her new, safe environment with lots of human TLC, good meals, long walks, play, her own doggie bed, and Kessie's friendship. It took three weeks, during which time she s-l-o-w-l-y responded; her head and tail came up, and her endearing floppy ears perked up in anticipation of walks and treats.

A few more weeks passed and the dogs were happy and bonded. Bob and Sandra planned an outing to Half Moon Bay to celebrate Kessie's birthday. On May 28, with Emma and Kessie happily romping on Dunes Beach, Bob proposed to Sandra. They were married at the Kohl mansion in Burlingame in October. Kessie and Emma served as the official ring bearers and were dressed for the occasion in flower wreathes and leashes wrapped in white satin. The reception featured lemonade, iced tea, and Martha Stewart-style dog cookies. Guest tables were identified by pictures of their dog friends. Bob and Sandra's wedding was later featured in *Bark Magazine*, and the main wedding picture captured the bride, groom, Kessie, and Emma.

As the years passed, Kessie lived on to celebrate her fourteenth birthday, and Emma learned to share her life with Sandra, Bob, three cats, a rabbit, various rescued golden and Labrador retriever foster dogs, and Cooper, another yellow Lab. Their lives together, with all animals in tow, included trips to the beaches and mountains for playing, hiking, swimming, sledding, and snowshoeing. Emma wore a red winter jacket and booties when needed. Awkward at first, she adopted quickly and soon preferred the booties instead of the accumulation of snowballs between her toes.

In her fifteenth year, Emma developed a lump, and Sandra, a licensed veterinary nurse, sought treatment. It was to no avail, and she died a year later of cancer. But Emma lived out the rest of her days in joy and companionship with Sandra and Bob, and they made the most of their time left together.

Sandra always loved Doris Day and respected her work as an animal advocate. So in July 2009, knowing Emma's days were short, she booked a room, packed up the car, and they traveled to Carmel for a special vacation. The Cypress Inn is a beautiful, dog-friendly, boutique hotel co-owned by Doris Day. Sandra and Emma enjoyed taking tea in the garden, dinner in the bar room, and reading in the great room. Most enjoyable were their strolls and talks on the beach, pictures taken, trying on silly hats in the pet stores, getting a bright, daisy-flowered bandana, sampling dog treats from the bakery, and snuggling up under a canopied, four-poster bed at night.

A week later, the family booked a room at the Ritz, and Emma sniffed the fresh, coastal air, enjoyed the beach, and caught up on her sleep. The next day she actually hiked Fort Funston in San Francisco and socialized with all the dogs. She died peacefully two days later.

Sandra and Bob shared their thoughts: "Our Miss Emma will be irreplaceable. We were so fortunate to share our lives with the most incredible dog—a rescued dog. She was gentle, kind, appreciative, and easygoing. Affectionate, she would put her face next to ours and lean into us for closeness. She followed us from room to room, wanting to share her last days with us. During our time together, she took as much care of us as we did of her. She was just a perfect dog. We're thankful for every day we spent with her during the past ten years. Thank you, Homeward Bound!"

Homeward Bound Golden Retriever Rescue and Sanctuary, Inc., founded in 2000, maintains an eight-acre sanctuary and adoption center in Elverta, near Sacramento. Homeward Bound (HB) is an all-volunteer organization of approximately 250 people dedicated to rescuing golden retrievers from shelters, owners who can no longer care for them, those found wandering the streets, and goldens reported by concerned neighbors. HB rescues the old, sick, injured, and healthy ones, as well as golden mixes when special circumstances arise. The sanctuary serves as a "halfway house" for those goldens awaiting adoption, and as a permanent home for those dogs whose health issues have rendered them unadoptable. Their facility includes a clinic area and approximately thirty professional-grade kennels. HB maintains close working relationships with animal shelters in Sacramento, Sutter, Placer, Yolo, El Dorado, and surrounding counties, as well as other shelters and rescue organizations throughout California and beyond. In 2009, more than 730 golden retrievers were rescued; approximately 4,160 were rescued from 2000 to 2008.

Special fundraising events by HB include the annual events Kibble & Bids, the Golf-Fore-Goldens Tournament, the Homeward Bound Reunion Picnic, and the Jamestown Golden Jubilee. Other fundraising opportunities include the Golden Mall, featuring one hundred stores by GoodSearch at http://www.GoodShop.com. A comprehensive quarterly newsletter and articles are posted online. For more information, visit http://www.homewardboundgoldens.org.

Stumpy Scores a Perfect Ten

Author's Note: *An English setter down on his luck with time running out had the great fortune to be adopted and trained by consummate setter owner/trainers. Paul and Sharen have had a total of thirteen Irish and English setters, eight of which were rescues. Paul sports a tattoo on his shoulder for Feather Run Blue Mist Sapphire, aka Doofie. Doofie was one of his previous setters and a love of his life.*

A rescue volunteer for Irish Setter Rescue named Paul was contacted by a concerned friend during a weekend in October 2004. An English setter was scheduled to be euthanized at the Contra Costa Animal Shelter the following Monday, and someone needed to rescue him. Paul was the only person available to help, and possibly the dog's last hope for survival. All of the English

Setter Rescue volunteers were attending their breed's dog show in Sacramento.

The shelter was a two-hour drive. Paul left early Monday morning and called ahead, requesting that personnel hold the dog until he arrived. There he found a terrified purebred male, a stray approximately seven years old, lying in a concrete run. Two bully dogs were in runs on either side of him, growling and trying to get to him through the wire fence. He was so stressed that he constantly drooled, and his coat was soaked in urine from lying in it. He was missing his right front leg and in such poor condition that Paul immediately signed the adoption paperwork and made plans to take him home. The puzzle was: why didn't his owner come for him? After all, someone had loved him and paid for his prior medical expenses regarding the surgery.

The setter was put in a crate and all the way home was as good as gold. Paul and his wife gave him a much-needed bath, but his coat began falling out in large clumps from the infections caused by the urine. That afternoon, the English Setter Rescue representatives called back, but they did not have a foster home available. It was decided that the dog would stay with them until a suitable forever home could be found. Paul decided to name him Stumpy, after the character that Walter Brennan played in a one of Paul's favorite John Wayne movies, *Rio Bravo*. Stumpy settled in for the night after a long and trying day.

The next day, Stumpy was taken to see Paul's veterinarian, Dr. Sue. She reported that the dog had been hit by a car and his shoulder shattered, resulting in the amputation of his right front leg. However, Stumpy was in good shape and would be healthy again with a good diet, antibiotics, and medicated shampoo.

Over the next few months, Stumpy settled in with Paul's family and his other setters. He got along with everyone and the stress disappeared. Stumpy constantly amazed them with his ability to get around. There was nothing he could not do as well as a four-legged dog: going up and down stairs, using the dog door, and, most startling of all, digging huge holes in the backyard! At times Paul would look out the window and see only his tail sticking up from a new hole that he had created.

Paul's household is "setter oriented" with a number of dog activities. He shows his setters in both confirmation and obedience. He also runs his dogs in field trials and hunt tests, as well as sponsoring field training events with his son, Scott, and friend, Carl. Paul brought Stumpy to all of the events so that he could meet more people and get exposure.

Paul related, "Everyone who ever met Stumpy immediately fell in love with him. Like us, they were amazed at what he could do."

In February 2005, he took Stumpy to a field trial. He had no intention of entering him, but at the last minute decided that as a "nonregular," it might be fun for him. Paul was not sure if Stumpy could even get around the entire course, but they tried anyway.

"On his first bird contact, he was not really sure what to make of this small creature hiding in the brush. On the second bird, he actually stopped for a moment and held a point. It was like a light went off in his brain, and all of the generations of pointing dogs were telling him what to do. On the third and fourth bird, he was rock solid on both points, like he had been doing it all of his life. He held until someone flushed the birds and fired a blank pistol shot. When the judges called time, I grinned from ear to ear. It took days to remove that grin off of my face!"

When the stake was over, the judges turned in their scores. Out of fourteen dogs, Stumpy was awarded third place, behind two exceptionally well-trained English setters. So began the start of Stumpy's field trial and hunting test career. Since he was a rescue dog, he could not run in AKC field trail stakes, but he ran in nonregular stakes, fun events, and the hunt test. He never failed to place in ribbons in any stake he competed in and won several first places along the way. He was so good that many owners did not want their dogs braced with him, for fear that a three-legged setter might make their dog look bad.

"He always gave me everything he had, but at the end of some stakes he would be so exhausted that I had to carry him out of the bird field. Sometimes he rode back slung over the judge's saddle. Everyone who ever saw him run was so impressed at how much heart and desire he possessed; it was like he found what God had put him on this earth for—to hunt for his handler and find and point birds."

Paul decided that perhaps Stumpy was ready for a try at junior hunter title. The first test they entered was a German shorthair test at Hasting Island Hunting Preserve in Central California. They left the line and Stumpy ran the course like he owned it, finding and pointing birds, holding steady to wing shot, and honoring his bracemates' points. At the end of his first junior hunter pass, he achieved scores of perfect tens, which are very difficult to achieve and seldom given. He qualified in every test that he entered, and never earning scores lower than nine. He was the talk of every event he entered.

Handlers and judges alike wanted to see how well Stumpy would compete as a senior hunter, but he was diagnosed with dysplasia in both hips at the age of nine, so his field trial career was cut short. However, Paul enrolled him in the fun events and stakes that were easy, so he could have a good time and enjoy himself.

Sadly, Stumpy passed away in March 2009. Paul shared his thoughts: "Stumpy was simply a joy to live with. There was never a complaint. He lived life every day to the fullest and taught everyone he met that a missing leg is never a liability. We had lots of quality time in the field together. He was a dog that I would have given anything to have gotten him when he was a puppy, been AKC registered, and had all four of his legs. He had field champion written all over him, but some things are just not meant to be. In the end, I learned more from him than he *ever* learned from me."

NorCal Irish Setter Rescue, Inc. (NCIS) was founded in 2000 and dedicated to the care and placement of their gentle, loving, red-headed friends by finding them permanent forever homes. They have approximately forty volunteers and rescue approximately thirty homeless dogs per year. Most Irish setters come out of county animal shelters and SPCAs, and most are in reasonably good health. Some dogs are owner-surrendered due to a change in lifestyle and, on rare occasion, abandoned. NCISR is based in the San Francisco Bay Area in Northern California and works closely with other rescue organizations to benefit Irish setters throughout the country. Special fundraising events include a St. Patrick's Day Parade in Dublin, California, the Irish Setter Club of the Pacific Fun-a-Fair, the Annual Rescue Reunion Picnic, and the Rescue Parade at the ISCP Specialty Dog Show. The NCIS newsletter, *Rescue Review,* is published quarterly and available online. For more information, visit http://www.ncisrescue.org.

From Katrina to Doggy Dancing

A dark, chocolate-colored pit bull with white patches and a missing tail survived Katrina's wrath in Louisiana in September 2005. The Louisiana SPCA organized an emergency center at the Lamar Dixon Expo Center in Gonzales, Louisiana. The pit bull and thousands of other rescued animals were temporarily kenneled there until other arrangements were made. Hundreds of rescue volunteers traveled from great distances to care for the animals, sleeping in cars, RVs, tents, cots, and floors.

The pit bull was then transferred over to the Dixon Correctional Institute (DCI), where he and other unclaimed Katrina pit bulls were housed in a prison shelter program for six months. It was at DCI that he was probably given the name of

Leroy and continued to live in a kennel. Dr. Lisa and Dr. Eric, local veterinarians, provided excellent care and supervision of inmates assigned to exercise and play with the dogs. Thankfully, with the help of the DCI staff, inmates, the Humane Society of the United States (HSUS), and Dr. Lisa and Dr. Eric, the dogs stayed healthy and sane after the storms in September.

In April 2006, seven months after Katrina, the founders of Bay Area Doglovers Responsible About Pit bulls (BAD RAP) received a grant from the HSUS. Donna and Tim endeavored to coordinate the rescue of twenty unclaimed pit bulls from Louisiana who were still at DCI.

Finally, the last of the Katrina dogs, including Leroy, were on the move! Six dogs were flown to three different states. Nine more were driven to their new locations and into waiting adoption programs. Several pit bull rescue organizations and shelters offered to take one to five dogs into their already-crowded rescue programs. Now the real work began with more medical care, training, socialization, and preparation of the healthy dogs for adoption. Some dogs had heartworm, which required weeks of confinement after their evacuation.

To his great fortune, Leroy was absorbed into BAD RAP's adoption program rescue and later moved into the Pit Bull Hall Project at the Oakland SPCA. It was there that he met Sara. Sara is a certified dog trainer and behavior counselor for BAD RAP, private clients, and various SPCAs. She knew exactly how to properly teach Leroy manners and introduce him to a leash and the world around him. She believes that he lived in Louisiana in a backyard by himself, tied up. His tail is a crooked stump, which is a mystery.

Sara said, "If Leroy had life experiences, they were not good ones. I'd put him on leash, and he jumped and rolled around. Just being on a leash was a huge training challenge for him. I taught him manners, how to go on walks, playing with toys, games, and tricks. He was smart and loved the human interaction and attention. He was very eager to learn new things and was puppy impulsive; lots of energy. I certified him as a Canine Good Citizen."

Leroy was in Pit Bull Hall for four months. He began to show signs of shelter weariness and anxiety, for it had been almost a year of living in a kennel. He needed much more human contact, companionship, and stability.

Then Sara's foster dog was adopted out and she brought him into her home as a foster dog. Leroy began to experience real growth and joy and a new world of human gadgets. Excited, he ran over to inspect everything: the can opener, wooden spoons, sunglasses, flip-flops, hats, towels, blankets, bathtub, television, cell phones, toilet paper, cookies, and doggy toys. He quickly bonded with his new pal, Widget, a Lab/shepherd mix, and Monkey the cat. It took only three days for Sara and her partner Jared to decide to officially adopt Leroy as their own.

Leroy's spirit is soaring at Sara and Jared's house. He plays with Widget and Monkey and any foster dog that Sara sponsors. He figures out dog puzzles with moving parts in record time to get his treats; he doggy dances with rocker moves of spins, weaves, and jumps. He headbangs with Sara in a dancing routine. Leroy loves wearing his own sweatshirt, T-shirt, sweater, and pajamas. And at bedtime, you guessed it—he sleeps under the covers with Sara and Jared.

Bay Area Doglovers Responsible About Pit bulls (BAD RAP) is based in Oakland and was founded in 1999. The organization consists of approximately fifty volunteers from around the Bay Area. Its mission is to secure the future of the American pit bull terrier as a cherished family companion. Committed to public education and training models for the breed, cofounders Donna Reynolds and Tim Racer have directed the nationally recognized Bit Bull Hall Project at the East Bay SPCA and the AmbassaDog Project at Oakland Animal Services. Through the Partners in Shelter Services Project, they assist progressive animal shelters in developing and activating their own pit bull adoption and public outreach programs. Pit Ed Camp is a week-long, breed-intensive workshop for shelter workers and earned the American Humane Association's 2006 Award for Best Practices in Behavior and Training. BAD RAP also offers free coaching classes to help intermediate handlers and their dogs pass the Canine Good Citizen Test, as well as dog safety classes to city employees that interact with dogs. Donna and Tim participated in evaluating the Michael Vick dogs in 2007.

BAD RAP's foster care program serves as a model for pit bull placement, as selected dogs are home fostered, trained, and socialized by pit bull-experienced volunteers like Sara. Once they are ready, dogs are offered for adoption to quality, breed-educated homes. Nearly 400 pit bulls and pit mixes have found forever homes. BAD RAP also supports other rescue efforts by offering free evaluations, training, and placement services.

Outreach events at pet fairs and other venues in the Bay Area feature demo dogs and a dedicated body of volunteers to handle the dogs and answer questions. Special fundraising events include a photo contest for the 2010 calendar and a barn raising campaign to build a halfway house for transitioning foster dogs. For more information, visit their Web site at http://www.badrap. org. Sara Scott, BAD RAP's AmbassaDog Trainer and a certified behavioral counselor for pit bulls, may be found at http://www. whatsupdogtraining.com.

A Second Chance for Scooter

Author's Note: *Dogs with amputated limbs can go on to lead happy, well-adjusted lives, and they have much to teach us about patience and resilience. Our thanks to the animal control officer, who personally intervened to save an injured dog.*

In the Central Valley's August heat in 2009, an animal control officer (ACO) responded to reports of a small dog that had been hit by a car. The officer found a severely injured stray weighing less than ten pounds. Grimy, bloody, and tick-infested, he had sustained a serious leg injury and in all probability was in severe pain and shock. But the cream-colored Eskimo terrier mix was friendly and good-natured, much to the officer's surprise.

The ACO knew that the Central Valley shelter could not offer the surgery needed to repair the dog's leg, and the dog would quickly be scheduled for euthanasia. He implored his personal veterinarian to come to the terrier's aid, and plans were made with the Valley Oak SPCA in Visalia to facilitate his placement. He then was treated for ticks and heartworm disease, and a veterinarian surgical team amputated the little guy's right front leg up to the shoulder. A few days later on August 17, the recuperating Eskimo terrier arrived at Tony La Russa's Animal Rescue Foundation (ARF) and was promptly named Scooter.

It became obvious that Scooter had much to teach to everyone, including Scooter's seasoned foster mom, Erika. Resilient, patient, fearless, and athletic, he quickly mastered how to walk on three legs—on his own! He figured out how to stand without a front limb, perfectly balancing his small frame by splaying out his back legs and slightly placing his one front leg underneath him. His long, fluffy tail curled to help support his body as well. Then Scooter learned to sit down and walk upright distances on his two hind legs, astounding Erika. In one week he taught himself how to walk down doggy stairs, which would be a complicated challenge with one front leg.

Erika, a foster mom to seventy-seven rescued dogs from ARF, shared her thoughts: "Scooter was *my baby*. *Best dog ever* out of all the dogs that I've fostered! I think that he loves everything, everyone, and every dog that he comes in contact with. He seems to be extremely grateful for his new life, and I think he understands that he was given a second chance.

"He is absolutely full of life and joyful all of the time. He really likes his balls and plays fetch; so much energy! Every dog he came in contact with while he was here at ARF was his friend, including a one-eyed Chihuahua. During a weekend, we took him to Clear Lake, and he charged right in. Fearless! So I held him and Scooter splashed happily, quickly wore himself out, and spent the rest of the day asleep on the dock in his bed. I don't think that it ever occurred to him that he couldn't dog paddle with one front leg."

Scooter was adopted in a matter of weeks by Matt and Michele in Walnut Creek. He now has a companion named Enzo, an Italian greyhound and Chihuahua mix who was also adopted from ARF.

Michelle reports, "Scooter keeps up with Enzo, which is amazing. He certainly is persistent; nothing is going to keep the little dog down. A lot of people are amazed by him, and he gets a lot of attention."

No doubt Scooter will continue to teach his owners and all the humans who have the pleasure to meet him valuable lessons about unconditional love and perseverance.

Animal Rescue Foundation (ARF) was founded in 1991 by Tony and Elaine La Russa to address the needs of companion animals. ARF saves abandoned, homeless, neglected, or abused dogs and cats in public shelters from euthanasia and brings animals and people together to enrich each others' lives. They embody a vision where animals are respected for the unique role they play to make the world a better place for people, and where there is a stable and loving home for every pet. More than two thousand dogs and cats were adopted into new and loving homes in 2009.

ARF has designed progressive programs for abused children, the elderly, victims of violence, and others who benefit from the healing contact of animals. ARF is a private, nonprofit organization with a state-of-the-art adoption and education center in a campus-like setting in Walnut Creek, California, and provides a home base for many special programs. Such programs are:

Maddie's Center (provides programs for animal care):

Adoption: Specialists work with potential adopters to create forever families.

Dog Training: ARF University offers classes for adopters and their new pets, as well as the general public.

Foodshare: Provides donated dog food, cat food, and litter to low-income residents of Contra Costa County.

Emergency Medical Fund: Provides veterinary care at ARF's clinic for pet owners who are low-income residents of Contra Costa County.

Guardian: What would happen to your companion animal if you are no longer here?

People Connect Center (provides programs promoting and fostering interaction between people and companion animals):

All Stars: Humane education and pet care courses for children regarding bite intervention, dog and cat behavior, and positive training reinforcements.

Camp ARF: A summer experience for children that strengthens the understanding and bond between children and animals.

Classes and Workshops: For all students and families stressing kindness and the humane treatment for all living creatures.

Learning Center: The first interactive center in the United States that teaches children about companion animals.

Pre-Teen and Teen Volunteer Training: For students in the middle grades and high school to become ARF volunteers.

TLC: An animal-assisted therapy program for young people with serious emotional and behavioral problems.

All Ears Reading: Supports literacy skill development by reading in a nonjudgmental environment to an ARF therapy animal.

Added Touch: For visitors from assisted living facilities to enjoy animal-assisted activities.

Pet Hug Pack: More than one hundred therapy animal teams make compassionate visits countywide to thousands of seniors in nursing homes and assisted living facilities and patients in hospitals or hospice.

Signature special fundraising events each year include Stars to the Rescue, Animals on Broadway, Paws on Parade, and Celebrities FORE! ARF. ARF's La Russa Boutique is located on their campus in Walnut Creek and features their celebrity pet calendar, clothing, caps and visors, gifts with ARF's logo, autographed items, and sports memorabilia. Their monthly newsletter, *Paws Press*, is available by e-mail and online. For more information, visit http://www.arf.net.

A Negotiation with God

Glenn has always been a lover of animals, but he hasn't always been involved in rescuing them. Champ, his golden retriever and a love of his life, was bought at a pet shop in a shopping mall. Most likely, Champ was the product of a puppy mill.

Years later, as Champ was battling cancer and gravely ill at the veterinarian's clinic, Glenn struggled to make the decision to end Champ's suffering and say good-bye. Despondent and knowing that he had to make the right choice for Champ, he found himself at another shopping mall. His inner voice drew him to a bookstore. There he spotted a picture of a flat-coated retriever on the cover of *Dog Fancy Magazine*, and he intuitively knew that this breed of dog would be his next.

Sadly, within a few hours, Champ passed away at the animal clinic before Glenn could say good-bye. Six months later he pursued his vision to own a flat-coated retriever. Kukui (meaning black nut in Hawaiian) was selected from a professional breeder. This dog was unusually handsome with a shiny, black, flat coat and a long and lean athletic body. But Kukui proved to be a barking "communicator" of sorts, and a neighbor complained. Something had to be done.

Glen decided that he needed to find a new house in the country, with lots of privacy and open space for another dog or two. His realtor showed him a perfect "bachelor pad" with a large backyard, and together they spent an hour inspecting the property. As he left, his inner voice told him to take a different route home. He soon found himself interested in a gated community, and it was there that he stumbled upon a large ranch for sale.

A big and bold plan began to form in his mind. He sighed. If he bought this property, he would surely leave his illustrious career of hotel and resort management and begin a new life of a different sort: animal rescue. Animal rescue literally dominated the lives of his father and his sister with projects called the Saint Francis Ranger Program and the Casa Pacific Equestrian Education Program (where disadvantaged children learn to ride horses), as well as Life Line for Paws (a private foundation that provides funds for medical procedures that canine rescue organizations cannot afford).

So began Glenn's negotiation with God: "Please, God, let me have ten more years in my career! I will make a lot more money, and I promise to give back in a huge way. I don't think I'm ready for the plan that you have for me now."

After days of contemplation and when he was finally at peace with his decision, he proceeded to buy the ranch property on fifteen acres. It needed work, and Glenn was prepared to rebuild and redesign the property to fit his grand scheme. For starters, roads needed to be repaved and a driveway built of concrete, all hills stabilized with retaining walls and proper landscaping, and a new barn for the animals had to be built.

Within an hour of closing escrow, Glenn received a frantic telephone call from a woman in Lancaster named Cynthia. She had recently lost her house to a fire, and she was unable to continue to care for her own rescued animals of four dogs and five horses. Cynthia was desperately seeking a new home for them; could he come and meet with her? Glenn did, and he took possession of her animals, all nine of them, within one day of taking ownership of the property.

The ranch already had the facilities for five horses, but not for Cynthia's four dogs. Since Glenn's vision included facilities for a large breed canine rescue, he set to work and built outdoor kennels. Initially the dogs enjoyed cooling off in the horse troughs, until Glenn bought them plastic kiddie pools. Then he built them a canine resort: a covered swimming pool in the shape of a bone with a fenced-in patio and yard that he calls "Co-paw Cabana." He now has comfortable facilities for twelve and cares for homeless dogs from the nearby communities of Camarillo, Newbury Park, Thousand Oaks, Westlake Village, Oak Park, and Agoura Hills. He's personally involved in each dog's rehabilitation and eventual adoption. Also, facilities for the original five horses were improved and expanded, and to date his sanctuary is home for thirty-five horses!

Rancho St. Francis is now a very special place for the healing of rescued animals *and* people. The ranch is a buzzing beehive of activity with ranch hands, volunteers, and docents who facilitate the needs of the animals and visiting children, teenagers, and adults who are physically and emotionally challenged. Some children have parents in the military serving overseas. Participating organizations include the Association of Retarded Citizens or ARC (from the cities of Camarillo and Ventura), Big Brothers, Big Sisters, Daybreak (a women's shelter in Santa Monica), and West View (an organization for adults with mental and physical challenges). Camarillo High School students, as well as students from several local colleges, volunteer as helpers and docents.

Visitors connect with the beautiful outdoor setting, enjoy themselves in a loving and safe environment, ride horses as therapy, and interact and care for the dogs, horses, and other animals: four cats, seven sheep, one mule, two donkeys, chickens, and ten mini horses! Landscaped grounds feature a waterfall, henhouse, sport court for horseshoes, and a "fruits of labor" garden. Security gates and a state-of-the-art infrastructure provide a private, safe sanctuary for the rehabilitation of both the animals and people.

Since Glenn's vision four years ago, Rancho St. Francis in Camarillo has come full circle. It's a very special place where animals rescue humans and humans rescue animals!

Big Paws 4 A Cause is a large breed rescue located on a fifteen-acre ranch in Camarillo, California. Their small staff is dedicated to enhancing the lives of neglected, abused, and abandoned dogs. Rehabilitation takes place in a safe, loving environment, and the end result is to find them appropriate forever homes. This organization focuses on caring for homeless dogs in the Southern California communities of Newbury Park, Thousand Oaks, Westlake Village, Agoura Hills, and Oak Park. Volunteer opportunities regarding the dogs include exercise, grooming, socialization, training, transportation for medical care, and fostering. A volunteer youth program is available for ages sixteen and seventeen. For more information about this organization, the adoption process, and volunteer opportunities, visit http://www.bigpaws4acause.org.

In Memory of a Very Sweet Girl

In the summer of 2008, a senior, shaggy-furred Rhodesian ridgeback and Chesapeake Bay retriever mix was dropped off anonymously at the San Francisco SPCA. She was thought to be ten to eleven years of age and very underweight. There was worry that she had health problems, which all but deemed her unadoptable. This SPCA maintains partnership with Muttville, a San Francisco rescue organization for senior dogs, and Sherri Franklin, the founder, was contacted in the hope of finding a home for a girl they named Goldie. The SPCA was happy to run the necessary medical tests to determine her health if Muttville could work on her placement and adoption to another family. In the meantime, Goldie would be more comfortable in a foster home until a permanent, loving home could be found.

Goldie was renamed Pretty Penny and went to live with Ali, her temporary foster mom. Her picture was placed on the Muttville Web site, and on November 1, her sweet face caught the attention of Alex, who was looking for a new canine companion. He was certainly interested in Pretty Penny but needed to know what medical problems existed before he adopted her. On November 14, x-rays and other tests confirmed that there was no growth in her lungs, as previously suspected. Alex and his friend Elmer drove up to San Francisco that night and picked her up. Her new life commenced in a beautiful Victorian house and garden in San Jose, California. This is a bittersweet account of Alex's life with Shaggy, featured with many pictures at his Web site http://alexvaz.com/shaggy:

> Shaggy quickly settled in quite nicely and got used to a routine within a few days. In the first week, she met many people, ran with my running group, participated in a Human Rights march, was the subject of many photographers, went to two dog parks, got her rabies shot, was fitted for a seat-belt harness, entertained us for an afternoon of board games, and began to eat *lots* of food. She learned a few commands and rules and was very eager to please. She loved to explore and gently moved things from the inside of the house to the outside or from room to room. At first the steps were difficult for her, and she often needed coaching or a helping hand.

> Shaggy was comfortable sleeping just about anywhere. She did not come to bed with me, so

I bought her an orthopedic mattress for her crate that she loved. During the day, she took naps around the house, following the sunshine. Her health got much better. The more weight she put on, the more her personality came out. I think that having more calories to spare got her mind to start functioning normally, and in some ways she became a six-month-old pup. She continued to run with me twice a week and went further and faster each time. She no longer needed the arthritis and joint medications. I suspected that she just didn't have enough muscle mass to walk properly and was misdiagnosed.

The holidays had me decorating and taking photos of my pooch for cards, an annual tradition. Shaggy slept all curled up in various positions, often with her long limbs crossed or folded. I realized that many of the photos showed her asleep because she rarely sat still long enough for me to snap a picture

Christmas brought Shaggy several new toys. Gumby and her old, blue Squeaky Bone were definitely her favorites. Squeaky was important because it came with her from her foster home, and Gumby because his head ripped off easily, and it was decidedly delicious!

One of her favorite things to do was to watch me and the neighbors work from various areas of the yard. She would, of course, always be a lady and cross her double-jointed legs. If we were inside, she became my shadow. This was rather annoying when I tried to vacuum or cook. She was great when I needed unconditional love, and she provided lots of that.

Her last few weeks were spent walking in the San Francisco Pride Parade with the Pets are Wonderful Support (PAWS) float, and various parties that included our birthday celebrations. She wore a rainbow boa for the parade and was photographed by everyone.

Shaggy's stomach turned in her belly at some point on July 15. Within hours she had a serious condition known as bloat. The only way to correct it was immediate surgery that had a low rate of success. Shaggy had been through a lot in her lifetime: an unknown past that brought her to the SPCA, then Muttville, and then to me. I couldn't put her through anything more. It all happened so fast. I left for a run, came home, and found her sick. She was gone two hours later.

I miss Shaggy so much, and will never forget the eight months of joy and laughter that she brought to me, her foster mom, Ali, and all of our friends.

Muttville was founded in 2007 by Sherri Franklin, a longtime animal advocate and rescue worker. Muttville is dedicated to improving the lives of senior dogs through foster, adoption, education, and community. This organization is one of only three in the United States that specifically rescues senior dogs and finds them new homes or provides hospice care. On a global level, they provide information about caring for older dogs and the support for people who do. Through associations with shelters and other animal organizations, Muttville finds senior dogs that have been given up and are not likely to find adopted homes. Through outreach and networking, they find suitable new homes for the dogs. Dogs come to Muttville from shelters as well as loving homes.

Sherri served six years as the vice chair of the Commission of Animal Control and Welfare for San Francisco. In 2004 she received the Guardian Award by In Defense of Animals. She continues to serve the community and address many animal-related issues, advising elected officials on animal-related legislation. Sherri continues to foster and hospice senior and special needs dogs for many organizations in the Bay Area.

The organization provides an e-newsletter and blog, Woofs: Daily Life at Muttville. Specially designed Muttville clothing and merchandise for humans and canines is also available online. Subscriptions may be purchased for news feeds concerning special fundraising events, Muttville news, and available dogs. For more information, go to http://www.muttville.org.

Parting Thoughts and Aha! Moments

This author would like to thank my new friends, the numerous canine rescue volunteers or Doers of Good, whose incredible stories made this publishing project possible. I soon learned that they are very busy people. We communicated at all hours during all the days of the week by telephone and e-mail. There were tons of leads, missed calls, unanswered messages, and vast spaces of time that passed without anyone available for an interview. It was my single focus, and it took me three months to call it a wrap.

It was truly a privilege to work with passionate individuals who find the time to rescue homeless dogs in the worst of circumstances, fix their medical and emotional problems, and place them into the best homes possible. Their sense of purpose and memories of their rescued dogs, both good and bad, seem to be stamped into their DNA. They walk canine rescue, talk canine rescue, and breathe canine rescue twenty-four hours a day, seven days a week. They recanted old memories as clearly as recent ones and recited old dialogues sentence by sentence. They made my job easy.

Many years ago I learned from my own experience as a rescue volunteer that perfect timing, inexplicable circumstances, and small miracles are not only commonplace but *can be expected*. Also, monies for dire emergencies such as surgeries and veterinarian care magically appear, and services are discounted or donated when desperately needed. In fact, virtually all of the rescue volunteers that I interviewed confirmed these things. Most people would call inexplicable circumstances "head shakers." Rescue organizations experience them as common occurrences!

When I conceived of this project, I wanted to find and convey these "head shaker" scenarios. I wasn't disappointed. My own "aha!" moment came after I finished story #26. I then realized that virtually all of the rescue tales included these inexplicable elements: a perfect pairing of dog to a rescuer, a perfect pairing of a dog to an owner, perfect timing that facilitates the rescue, puzzling circumstances that lead to a positive outcome, and the miracle of life in the face of death.

A movement of animal advocacy has been gaining momentum for many years, bringing "aha!" enlightenment to people all over the world. Did you know that Animal Planet, a satellite and cable television channel, has syndication in Europe, Asia, Latin America, Japan, and Canada? Cesar Millan, a featured dog trainer on Animal Planet, may lead the pack as a high-profile animal advocate, but he is joined by Hollywood celebrities like Doris Day, Linda Blair, Pamela Anderson, Bob Barker, Kelsey Grammer, Hilary Swank, Kim Basinger, Katherine Heigl, and Ellen DeGeneres. Ellen recently partnered with the U.S. Postal Service in a campaign called "Stamps to the Rescue." When the public buys stamps in commemoration of animal rights, Ellen's pet food company will purchase food for one million shelter pets. Wow!

I particularly want to mention to you that this movement wouldn't be what it is today without corporate partners. On any given weekend, adoption events are held throughout California and the rest of the nation in PETCOs, PetSmarts, and other pet product stores supporting grassroots rescue organizations and their programs. Millions of dollars and vast amounts of pet food are donated each year, thanks to their foundation fundraisers! Also, virtually all of the major pet food companies have public relations campaigns to benefit animal advocacy, which you see in advertisements on television and rescue Web sites. And last but not least, there is petfinder.com, which provides a searchable database of animals that need homes from more than nine thousand animal shelters and adoption agencies in the United States, Canada, and Mexico. They have helped find homes for more than ten million pets!

It was indeed a pleasure and an honor to work with twenty-six outstanding California canine rescue organizations. My vision is to continue the DOG (Doers of Good) series into the next decade, promoting organizations from all fifty states. If you are a canine rescue volunteer and have a special story that you would like to share with me, please visit my Web site at http://www.doersofgood.com.

I hope that you will consider getting involved in animal rescue in any way that you can. There is a list of volunteer job descriptions and what they entail in the introduction of this book. It could be as simple as helping with a fundraising event, writing a newsletter, exercising dogs, assisting with adoption events on weekends, or just writing a check.

My own involvement with canine rescue had a profound effect on me. I will never forget their sad eyes, the grime and smell of their incarceration, and the way that they insisted on being near me by sitting in the passenger seat of my Jeep or draping themselves over the center console to lie in my lap. A loving touch was important. I kept one hand on the steering wheel, while the other hand gently stroked their heads and shoulders. The routine included calm music from my favorite CD, blankets, bottled water, dog biscuits, air-conditioning, and a conversation with them that went something like this:

> You're going to be okay. You're safe. I'm taking you to someone who will take care of you. Did you know that you're very special? You are loved. Rest.